honey for a child's heart

honey for a child's heart

*The imaginative use of books
in family life*

by GLADYS HUNT

Introduction by Dr. Frank E. Gaebelein

ZONDERVAN PUBLISHING HOUSE
Grand Rapids, Michigan

To
Mark,
a delightful companion
in adventures

Books are like people:
    fascinating, inspiring, thought-provoking,
some laugh,
some meditate,
    others ache with old age, but still have wisdom;
some are disease-ridden,
some deceitful;
    but others are a delight to behold,
and many travel to foreign lands;
some cry, some teach, others are lots of fun.
    they are excellent companions,
and all have individuality —
Books are friends.
What person has too many friends?

Introduction

Few things are more important for a child than to discover the joy of reading. Give him a love of reading, and you have given him not only the most satisfying and useful of all recreations but also the key to true learning. The home is still the greatest educational force, and parents who make reading attractive contribute immeasurably to their children's intellectual, emotional, and spiritual development. Forty-one years as a headmaster have convinced me that a genuinely educated person is one who knows how to read and who keeps on reading throughout his life. As Matthew Arnold said, "Culture is reading."

In *Honey for a Child's Heart*, Gladys Hunt has written a small book with a big potential. Her suggestions will do much to lift the cultural level of many a Christian home. Moreover, her practical and lively discussion of the place of the Bible in the family tells how parents can help children gain a life-long love for Scripture. What she says about reading aloud all sorts of literature brings memories of many a Sunday evening in my home at Stony Brook when, after chapel, boys crowded our living room as I read to them before the open fire.

Mrs. Hunt's tastes are broad. Her prose suggestions, which include A. A. Milne, Hugh Lofting, and Lois Lenski, range from Bunyan and Defoe through Dickens, Kipling, and Stevenson to C. S. Lewis, Conan Doyle, Buchan, E. B. White, Thurber and Tolkien. Among her poetry recommendations are Lear, Blake, Masefield, Sandburg, and Frost.

In writing this guide to the enjoyable use of books in family life, Gladys Hunt may well have made herself the benefactress of many a home. And if my enthusiasm for her persuasive little book encourages parents to act upon its advice, I shall be happy indeed.

FRANK E. GAEBELEIN

Arlington, Virginia

Contents

Bequest of Wings

Pooh and Piglet nearly catch a Woozle.

1

Bequest of Wings

"I'M GOING TO PLAY in the Hundred Acre Wood," said the small boy who lived at our house.

I knew what he meant and where he was going, and so I said, "Fine. If you see Owl, be sure to ask him about Eeyore's tail."

We knew about Eeyore, Pooh, Piglet, Owl and Christopher Robin. We had met them in a book[1] together and our life would always be richer because they had become our friends. To this day I feel sorry for anyone who hasn't made their acquaintance.

---

[1]A. A. Milne, *Winnie the Pooh*.

That is what a book does. It introduces us to people and places we wouldn't ordinarily know. A good book is a magic gateway into a wider world of wonder, of beauty, of delight and adventure. Books are experiences that make us grow, that add something to our inner stature.

Children and books go together in a special way. I can't imagine any pleasure greater than bringing to the uncluttered, supple mind of a child the delight of knowing God and the many rich things He has given us to enjoy. This is every parent's privilege, and books are his keenest tools. Children don't stumble onto good books by themselves; they must be introduced to the wonder of words put together in such a way that they spin out pure joy and magic.[2]

I used to have an eloquent old journalism professor who would often exclaim rapturously, "Oh the beauty and mystery of words! What richness can be conveyed by those who master them!" And while we jokingly recounted his dramatic incantations to our friends, we ourselves coveted the mastery of words, the symbols which convey ideas. We knew that what he said was true.

Take all the words available in the human vocabulary and read them from the dictionary and you have only a list of words. But with the creativity and imagination God has given human beings, let these words flow together in the right order and they give wings to the spirit. Every child ought to know the pleasure of words so well chosen that they awaken sensibility, great emotions and understanding of truth. This is the magic of words — a touch of the supernatural, communication which ministers to the spirit, a gift of God.

We cannot underestimate the use of words in creative thought! Proverbs says, "A word fitly spoken is like apples of gold in pictures of silver." The right word in the right

---

[2]Magic: Any extraordinary or irresistible influence. *The Random House Dictionary*.

place is a magnificent gift. Somehow a limited, poverty-stricken vocabulary works toward equally limited use of ideas and imagination. On the other hand, the provocative use of the right words, of a growing vocabulary gives us adequate material with which to clothe our thoughts and leads to a richer world of expression.

What fun it is to encourage a personal awareness of words in a child — the delight of sound, the color and variety of words available to our use. I am not suggesting vocabulary drills which teach by rote the meaning of large words. That is quite different than feeling the beauty of words. Books, the right kind of books, can give us the experience of words. They have power to evoke emotion, a sense of spiritual conviction, an inner expansion that fills a child to the brim so that "the years ahead will never run dry."

Books and experience go together. I delight in remembering the night we stayed late after a family picnic along an isolated lake in the north woods — far past normal bedtime for children. We watched the rosy glow of the sunset color the sky on the far side of the lake and darken the silhouettes of the trees. We felt the sand shed its warmth and take on a damp coolness. And then darkness came. We sat around the campfire and listened to the sounds of the night. Young ears picked up things older ears hadn't heard. What we heard we tried to express in words.

Deep-voiced bullfrogs far away, anxious peepers closer by, the gentle lap of the water on the shore, the loon crying in the distance, the crackle of the wood in the fire, the sparks going upward like brief fireflies. And then, as though it were a special gift from God, a whippoorwill, a shy bird usually heard only from a distance, lighted in the bush just behind us and startled us with his clarity of song. Later we watched the moon rise over the trees before going home. We felt Beauty, we heard and saw it. We tried to couch the experience in words. Chatter does not enrich; the right words do. Well-chosen words need only be few in number and they help store away the pleasure of the adventure.

We have often awakened a small boy at midnight to see the marvel of the northern lights. We have stood on hillsides and described the numerous shades of springtime greens across the landscape. It's a marvelous game of awareness and words.

It's a game that can be played anywhere at odd moments. *How do you think a barn in Nebraska looks?* One child may answer, "Red, with cows around it." Another may say, "Gray and lonely, with no trees near." A third child may light up and say, "The barn looks gray and tired, weathered from the summer's blast of heat and weary from icy winds that blow across the flat plains in winter."

Each answer is a good one. Yet those who saw less will be pleased by the contributions of those who saw more in their minds. They will sense the living substance of a touch of imagination and try to increase their own awareness. You may be thinking at this point, *I handle words so poorly my-self. How can I help my children?* This game will teach you as well, and bind you to your children as you share what we call "imaginings."

Try other questions: How does a summer night sound? How does a rainy day feel? What does a kindergarten child look like on her way home from school? I have done this in the classroom. Some children's contributions were cloddish and uninspired, some were hopeful, others had the bright shine of originality. But each child saw the "possibility of words." Natural gifts may differ and, like any other game, contributions should never be the only measure of a person's success. This is only one way of animating the mind in creative effort. But it will help train the ear to listen and the heart to feel beauty and emotion as it comes out in stories that the children later read. The benefits work both ways.

Reading aloud with two teen-age boys this summer, we discussed together the elements of writing which made the story so special. They went back through the chapter and found phrases that spelled out beauty like this, ["I feel like Spring after winter, and sun on the leaves; and like trumpets and harps and all the songs I have ever heard!"] The words fairly ring with joy! I covet for both of these boys the ability to use language with the mastery of the author (Tolkien) whose book we were reading.

Since words are the way we communicate experiences, truth and situations, who should know how to use them more creatively than Christians? [The world is crying out for imaginative people who can spell out truth in words which communicate meaningfully to people in their human situation.] Of all people on earth, committed Christians ought to be the most creative for they are indwelt by the Creator. [Charles Morgan speaks of creative art as "that power to be for the moment a flash of communication between God and man." That concept opens up our horizons to a glimpse of God-huge thoughts, of beauty, of substance beyond our cloddish earthiness, of the immensity of all there is to discover.

Yet, tragically, Christians often seem most inhibited and poverty-stricken in human expression and creativity. Part of this predicament comes from a false concept of what is true and good. The fear of contamination has led people to believe that only what someone else has clearly labelled *Christian* is safe. Truth is falsely made as narrow as any given sub-culture, not as large as God's lavish gifts to men. Truth and excellence have a way of springing up all over the world, and our role as parents is to teach our children [how to find and enjoy the riches of God and to reject what is mediocre and unworthy of Him.

Children are the freest and most imaginative of creatures. They love the fun of words and have a spectacular ability to learn. We must respect their eagerness and competence by introducing them to good books. I am frankly excited by the potential of books to build a whole, healthy, spiritually alert child who has the capacity to enjoy God and be useful to Him.

Emily Dickinson has winsomely captured the spirit of this,

> He ate and drank the precious words,
> His spirit grew robust,
> He knew no more that he was poor,
> Or that his frame was dust.
> He danced along the dingy ways
> And this bequest of wings
> Was but a book. What liberty
> A loosened spirit brings![3]

Any good book can be used by God in a child's development, for a good book has genuine spiritual substance, not just intellectual enjoyment. Books help children know what to look for in life. It is like developing the taste buds of one's mind as a child learns to savor what he sees, hears and experiences and fits these into some kind of worthwhile framework.

What is unfamiliar becomes close and real in books. What is ridiculous helps children see the humor in their own lives. Sympathetic understanding is a generous by-product of sharing the emotions of others in stories. Books are no substitute for life, but a keener pleasure comes to life because of books.

When you've walked across a field with an eight-year-old who comments on the "smell of sweet grass in a sunny pasture," then you'll understand what I mean. Or "Dandelion stems are full of milk, clover heads are loaded with nectar and the refrigerator is full of ice-cold drinks. Summer is very nice." Then you hear the words you read from *Charlotte's Web* come back to your own daily experience and agree, "Yes, summer is very nice."

This savoring of life is no small thing. The element of wonder is almost lost today with our mechanical devices and space age living. [To let a child lose it is to make him blind

---

[3] *The Poems of Emily Dickinson*, Crowell p. 20.

and deaf to most of life. Children have marvelous elasticity of mind. Fancy a child who hasn't met a dragon or a unicorn! Imagine a child who doesn't speculate about what small creatures might live in a hollow tree or rocky crevice! That's the stuff a sense of wonder may feed on, but when the child is older he will respond with the same sensitivity to a lovely sentence from Monica Shannon's *Dobry*: "Snow is the most ←
beautiful silence in the world."

I have never been able to resist the appeal of a child who asks, "Read to me, please?" The warm security of a little person cuddled close, loving the pictures which help tell the story, listening to the rhythm of the words, laughing in all the right places as the policeman stops Boston traffic for the mother duck and her family in Robert McCloskey's *Make Way for Ducklings*. Or the safe, soothing feeling of Margaret Wise Brown's *Good Night Moon*, or the wonder of Alvin Tresselt's *White Snow, Bright Snow*.

But the pleasure doesn't end with small children who like to sit on your lap. Growing-up children are just as much fun. Reading Laura Ingalls Wilder's books of pioneer adventure on the prairie, our family could feel the warm cabin, smell the freshly baked bread, hear the blizzard raging outside, and experience with Laura the close family feeling of Pa's singing and fiddling by the fireside. The love and gaiety of the Ingalls home was shared in our home and we had a quiet confidence in a family's ability to surmount dangers and hardships.

Books *do* impart a sense of security. Children meet others whose backgrounds, religions and cultural ways are unlike their own. They come to accept the feeling of being different and fear, which is the result of not understanding, is removed. Geography invades our living rooms as children visit families from other countries, and the world seems quite friendly.

Facing failures and tragedies with the characters of a story may vicariously give children the experience of courage and loyalty. Weeping with some and rejoicing with others — this is the beginning of a compassionate heart.

Courage is transmitted by heroes like *Johnny Tremain* and even the comical Reepicheep in *The Voyage of the Dawn Treader*. Valor does not belong to an exclusive race of supermen. It is within the heart of those who are committed to truth and honor, the kind of hero with whom one can identify. Children have loved the biblical Daniel, David, and Joseph for these same reasons and have seen deeper truths of the relationships of courage to faith.

One of my young friends read *Call It Courage* at least four times last year when he was nine. In transition between being a *child* and being a *boy*, he needed a model for his new manhood. [This book fed his heart with ideals and integrity in such practical ways that it is difficult to measure its influence.] He said, "It made me feel brave and strong!"

Every parent who reads with children and every teacher who shares books knows the wistful sigh that accompanies the request for "one more chapter." Because I loved reading so much myself I can never be too harsh when asked, "May I just finish this chapter?" even when I suspect that they are only on page two. I remember with special fondness the English teacher in my high school who sat on the corner of her desk and enchanted us with the music of Sir Walter Scott's *Lady of the Lake*,

> The stag at eve had drunk its fill,
> Where danced the moon on Monan's rill,
> And deep his midnight lair had made
> In lone Glenartney's hazel shade . . .[4]

Later as a teacher myself, I knew the delight of taking children into a great adventure with a story, of the utter silence of the room, the intent look on the children's faces and the involuntary sigh that escaped our lips at the conclusion of

---

[4]Sir Walter Scott, *The Lady of the Lake*, Macmillan.

the episode. [We had been together in the presence of good writing, and we felt bound together by the experience.] My sojourn in that school was brief, but only recently a former student met me unexpectedly and eagerly told me what book she was reading. She could have paid me no greater compliment. Great literature has a way of building people. Books continue to be an influence far beyond my own words to these children.

What I am saying is simply this: As Christian parents we are concerned about building whole people — people who are alive emotionally, spiritually, intellectually. The instruction to *train up a child in the way he should go* encompasses so much more than teaching him the facts of the Gospel. It is to train the child's character, to give him high ideals and to encourage integrity. It is to provide largeness of thought, creative thinking, imaginative wondering — an adequate view of God and His world. He can never really appreciate the finest without personal redemption. But many a redeemed person lives in a small insecure world because he has never walked with God into the larger place which is His domain. We have books and The Book at our disposal to use wisely for God's glory.

A young child, a fresh uncluttered mind, a world before him — to what treasures will you lead him? With what will you furnish his spirit?

Milk and Honey

Playing Pooh sticks.

2

Milk and Honey

SOMETIME AGO I borrowed a number of children's books from a friend whose family enjoys good books. When I returned them several days later, their three-year-old Jim welcomed back this familiar stack and carefully went through the books, his face lighting up with pleasure as he came upon favorites. Finally he found the special one he was looking for and hugged it to himself and said, "I *like* this one!" He was greeting an old friend.

He sat down to look through it, reciting the phrases which were dear to him, laughing at some pages, earnestly studying others. Even the size and the feel of the book seemed important to him, a prized possession.

Books were important to Jim because they were to his

parents. He hears his mother and father talk about books at the dinner table. His parents take time out to read to him. Books are always treated with respect and care. None of the four children in this family have been permitted as babies to take old magazines and destroy the pages. It isn't proper respect for a book; books are handled with care and placed back on the shelf. In turn, each of the children have looked forward to the day when they could read and enter into the private, special world of books on their own.

Parents unconsciously teach their children what is valuable by the way they spend their own time. If television is more important to the parent than books, the children will likely choose the same. If the caliber of television and its advertising was consistently excellent, then perhaps less would be lost. Television is here to stay and its better productions are highly recommended learning experiences. Certainly it would be folly for me in one paragraph to try to defeat the allurements of the screen. But families do have to repeatedly make conscious decisions about what is valuable and then choose the best over the mediocre. If appreciation of beauty and the gift of articulation are meaningful to you, then I suggest that exposure to great writing is a necessity.

The choice will sometimes be a clean house with the television as morning baby sitter, or a partially clean house, no telephone conversations, and a half hour of sharing a picture book. Or father might choose to delay the relaxation of reading his newspaper to make time for a story with the children.

A busy schedule is the enemy of reading. Agreeing in principle with all the benefits of books, you may at this point simply sigh and say, "I wish we had more time for reading." But the fact remains that we arrange time for what we think is truly important. Perhaps some other activities will have to be curtailed — committees, hobbies, clubs, church meetings, a wife's job — in order to free you to do what you decide is right to do.

A Swiss friend visiting in the States remarked about the telephone as the great intruder into American life. "Wherever I go," he said, "no matter how important a conversation, a prayer, a Bible reading, a peaceful dinner gathering, Americans willingly let the telephone interrupt whatever they are doing. It is as if they think God is calling!" An astute observation. We take the telephone off the hook or shut off the bell when we do not wish our family times trespassed. If the line is busy, important calls are dialed again at later intervals. For some things the world can wait! ←⎯⎯⎯⎯⎯

Nowhere in the New Testament are we encouraged to follow each other like a herd of thoughtless animals, pushed about by life. We have freedom and capacity to choose. God's promise of wisdom to those who ask is given on the condition that the person [open himself up to God's ideas and be ready to obey.] I have a painful feeling that family life is often more obedient to a given sub-culture than to the Lord of Glory. Each set of parents is charged with responsibility for their children. Each must *choose* goals which they deem valuable, and then make private decisions to implement them. Life seems full of choices between good, better and best. Only lazy parents avoid making decisions. And remember, parents bend the twig long before it gets to the school teacher.

The plea I am making is simply this — make time for books! Don't let your children live in spiritual poverty when abundance is available!

Erich Fromm in his book *The Art of Loving* speaks of a child's basic need for *milk* and *honey* from his parents. *Milk* is the symbol of the care a child receives for his physical needs, for his person. *Honey* symbolizes the sweetness of life, that special quality that gives the sparkle within a person. Fromm says, "Most mothers are capable of giving milk, but only a minority of giving honey, too." To give honey, one ← must love honey and have it to give. Good books are rich in honey.

⌐ A wise philosopher in James Stephen's *The Crock of Gold*
says, "I have learned . . . that the head does not hear anything until the heart has listened, and what the heart knows
today the head will understand tomorrow." What a reservoir
∟of wisdom good literature can store away for the heart!

What kind of books are proper fare for a child's mind?
Discovering these will lift your own heart and give you a taste
for honey. Once you begin enjoying good children's literature you will find yourself in a treasure house of reading.
Take care in your new eagerness not to push your child into
books beyond his years. While he may love them, it simply
means he'll miss the books tailored just for his present years.

What kind of books? "Stories that make for wonder. Stories that make for laughter. Stories that stir one within with
an understanding of the true nature of courage, of love, of
beauty. Stories that make one tingle with high adventure,
with daring, with grim determination, with the capacity of
seeing danger through to the end. Stories that bring our
minds to kneel in reverence; stories that show the tenderness of true mercy, the strength of loyalty, the unmawkish
respect for what is good."[1] A good book is always an experience containing spiritual, emotional and intellectual di-
mensions.

Picture books are a child's first introduction to the world
of reading. He *reads* pictures. A little child expects the
pictures to tell the story and to tell it accurately. Who can
know all the impressions and data he stores up in his private
world from a picture book? Such books provide the fun of
looking, but they also give an experience. By sharing their
own observations, parents teach their children how to look
at pictures.

Some concept of art values will begin to form in the child's
mind as he looks at pictures. Don't take the illustrations in a

---

[1] Ruth Sawyer, *The Way of the Storyteller*, Viking Press, p. 157.

book lightly. If a book which says good things has illustrations which are stiff and stereotyped, use the book anyway. You will be buying other books which contain really good illustrations as a child grows older. Exposing him to a variety in art helps him to choose what he likes. Make a point of commenting on colors and artistic expression to help him *see*. The book listing in the appendix has notations after the book title of outstanding illustrators.

However, a warning. Your view of art may not always be a child's view of pleasing art. I'm thinking particularly of some of the artwork done by Illustrator Maurice Sendak, a favorite with children. Something of the child in me responds to his hilarious drawings. But librarians gasped in horror when *Where the Wild Things Are* was chosen as a Caldecott Award winner. One children's librarian told me she was appalled and was certain children would reject it. To her surprise there was a raid on every copy in the library. The book never stands idle on the shelf.

Why did the children like it so much? Because Sendak pictured what they would have drawn in the story of rebellious Max and his adventure with the Wild Things. Mr. Sendak has been deluged with drawings sent to him by children, their own creations of Wild Things.

Ursula Nordstrom in an article in *Saturday Review* tells of one four-year-old in a day-care center in Brooklyn who would not speak except for an occasional indistinct utterance. She was apathetic and unresponsive. Slow improvement began to appear in the storytelling time, and when the teacher chose *Where the Wild Things Are* the child listened and looked intently. Afterward she approached the teacher and uttered her first sentence, "May I have that book?" Something in that book opened up a needy little girl, who has since become an avid lover of books and an affectionate child.

Many times children say, "Now I'll read you this story," and then proceed to read what the pictures are saying. Or, have you ever had your child say, "Don't read the writing,

Snow is to roll in

Buttons are to
keep people warm

From *A Hole Is to Dig* by Ruth Krauss, illustrated by Maurice Sendak. Copyright © 1952, as to text, by Ruth Krauss. Copyright © 1952, as to pictures, by Maurice Sendak. Reprinted with permission of Harper & Row, Publishers.

read the pictures." Begin to notice illustrators you and your children like and look for their work. (Incidentally, some artists change their style over a period of time. Mr. Sendak's more recent illustrations are not nearly as happy and light as his earlier ones.)

Kinds of Books

The best Christian children's books are for younger boys and girls. When children become avid readers of adventure stories on their own, the distinctly Christian market has far less quality to offer. Publishers have fussed over this problem, but I am not too disturbed because when we try too hard we end up with false concepts of sacred and secular. I believe God uses good children's books and insist that quality has high priority.

C. S. Lewis' children's books stand in a class apart for excellence. Paul White's *Jungle Doctor* books also affirm that Christian fiction can achieve a high standard, as do the books of Patricia St. John. (And don't forget the books of George MacDonald.) After these, the list of superior writers of what we call "Christian" fiction for children dwindles. The books I have mentioned are special, but general publishers of children's books have others that communicate values which are thoroughly Christian, if not overtly so. Generally it is better to acquaint your child with a book of quality than with second-rate writing where the plot is only a thin disguise for dumping the Christian message. Children have a precocious skill for skipping paragraphs, pages and whole chapters if they feel a sermon coming, says Paul Hazard in his classic work on children's books.[2]

But for the years when parents most need creative instructional help in teaching their children, good books are not hard to find. Notice carefully those especially listed under *Family Teaching* in the appendix. Some of the *Pattibooks*

---

[2]Paul Hazard, *Books, Children and Men*, Horn Books.

are good nursery age books with heavy, soil resistant pages. Joan Thomas' books have delicate illustrations. *Fairest Lord Jesus* tells the story of Jesus for beginners. The *Arch books* have become immensely popular with children. Each tells a Bible story.

Every family should investigate the selection of complete Bible story books and choose one. Apart from these it is easy to recount only the more popular Bible stories instead of getting the sweep of Scripture.

As Christians the most important message we have to communicate to our children is about God, who He is and what He has done. He loves us, listens to us and cares about our lives. If God is important to you, this will become a most vital part of your sharing with your children and you will use every helpful means to give instruction on this level.

But that's only the beginning. The whole world of things God made or let man discover is waiting for a child in books.

On our book shelves stand twenty-three small volumes of the works of Beatrix Potter. The copyright dates are in the early 1900's, but I expect them to be as popular with our great-grandchildren as with our children. Her picture stories should be among the first owned by a child for his own personal library. Her illustrations are timeless, an inseparable part of her stories; her characterizations are brief, but ever so lucid. Your children simply must meet Peter Rabbit, Johnny Town Mouse, Squirrel Nutkin, Jemima Puddleduck, Jeremy Fisher and other unforgettable characters.

It was from Miss Potter that I first learned how much children love big words. Miss Potter's economy of words — she chooses just the right one while other authors might require many — give liveliness to her stories, but every so often she tucks in a gem of a new word for children to roll over their tongues. The sparrows in *The Tale of Peter Rabbit* "implore him to exert himself" when he is caught in a net by his jacket buttons. The gentleman fox in *The Tale of Jemima Puddleduck* is "hospitable" and speaks of Jemima

Jemima shares her troubles with the gentleman fox.

"commencing her tedious setting on the eggs," and Jemima herself complains of a "superfluous" hen who is too lazy to do so.

Does this turn children off? No, seemingly not. I gathered my conclusions when I heard our own small child *implore* one of his friends to *exert himself.* Dr. Seuss makes the most of a child's fascination with words in his books, devising words from out of his imagination that delight children, regardless of what adults think of them. Could it be that all words belong to children as much as to adults?

Families grow a good deal together by discovering the fun of words. Happy is the home that has one parent at least who says, "Let's look it up!" and helps children to see that a dictionary is a fascinating friend. I remember the day "ubiquitous" occurred in something we read aloud together and with what pride that word became part of our household vocabulary.

Maybe you have wondered about the wisdom of fairy stories in your child's life. I heard a man recently say that life wasn't really like *Cinderella* and that wicked stepmothers who want to kill beautiful daughters aren't the best fare for the mind. Others don't like elves and fairies and talking animals. Some refuse even Santa Claus.

You'll have to make up your own mind, but I, for one, like *Cinderella* and elves and talking animals and even Santa Claus. Children don't take life as seriously as adults and are more inclined to read for pleasure without theorizing until all the fun is wrung out. Fairy stories don't condone poor behavior; they simply relate what occurs. Children learn very early that there are good people, bad people, kind people, cruel people and assortments of behavior in-between. And children have room in their lives for all sorts of miracles.

That's the problem, someone will say. If you let them believe in fairies and fantasy, how will they distinguish between truth and falsehood? I can't help thinking that since children love make-believe, they can easily tell the difference. We have wondered if the silvery, dewey spider webs in the early morning sun had been part of the decorations for a ball the fairies held the night before, especially if some toadstools had sprung up in the same area. We discussed it as if it were true, but it was like sharing a special secret. We all knew it was make-believe. There is nothing unspiritual about an active imagination, a token of the liberty of childhood.

One of my young friends at three told me about the tiger who lived in her backyard. I inquired about where she kept him and what she fed him, and she told me the details with great delight. Then I told her about the tiger who lived in *my* backyard. Her eyes danced as I described his strange behavior. Then she came very close and whispered, "Is yours a real one?" When I said it wasn't, she said confidentially, "Mine isn't either."

Was I encouraging her to lie? I think not. Both of us were in on the world of pretend — a legitimate adventure. How quickly we want to quench the fine spirit of childhood. Imagination is the stuff out of which creativity comes, and this little girl's art work already shows a skillful amount of this rare ingredient.

Our ten-year-old was in on a discussion with university students travelling along in a car together. One student said he would never tell his child about Santa Claus because when he found out he wasn't real maybe the child would conclude Jesus Christ wasn't real either. After listening to the debate, our son came up with his contribution. "I knew about Santa Claus, like I knew about elves and other pretend things. I never got him mixed up with the Lord Jesus because I could tell from the way my parents talked and acted all year long that Jesus was true."

If your experience has been different, perhaps we should only conclude that there are a number of variables of personality, emphasis and other intangibles which might make it so. C. S. Lewis once commented "that we who still enjoy

Drawing by E. H. Shepard from *Winnie the Pooh* by A. A. Milne.
Copyright, 1928, by E. P. Dutton & Co., Inc. Renewal, © 1956
by A. A. Milne. Reproduced by permission of the publishers.

fairy tales have less reason to wish actual childhood back. We have kept its pleasures and added some grown-up ones as well."

A. A. Milne's *Winnie the Pooh* and *The House at Pooh Corner* are examples of some of the finest kind of fantasy — the kind which is ageless. One small child asked, "Are you reading a children's book or am I reading a grown-up book?" because that's the way *Winnie the Pooh* is. It's full of talking animals with lovable personalities and exceedingly humorous situations, for which age only increases appreciation.

Which brings us to the subject of humorous stories: a child's reading should be sprinkled with them. From the ludicrous situation of *Horton Hatches an Egg* to the more subtle humor and wisdom of *The Wind in the Willows* to the simpler boyish adventures of *Homer Price* and *Henry Huggins* or the magical girl who lived with a horse and a monkey named *Pippi Longstockings* — give your child large doses of these. Some nonsense is good for everyone, like the unforgettable tea party in *Alice in Wonderland*.

As children grow older they will enjoy tales of courage (*Call it Courage, The Matchlock Gun*), stories about animals (*King of the Wind, Bambi,* a book which is usually read too young in a popularized version), adventure stories (*Caddie Woodlawn, Kon-Tiki*) and a wealth of experience in mysteries (*The Adventures of Sherlock Holmes, Adventures of Richard Hannay.*) Biographies, epic hero tales and historical novels are all part of rounding out the reading picture.

Children grow up hearing about classics and some are conditioned against them because they feel that surely dullness and classic must go together. Sometimes this is because books we call classics are introduced poorly or too early. I prefer to call them "good books." They are classics because they have demonstrated the enduring qualities of good literature (discussed in Chapter 3); therefore to cheapen or simplify them for popular reading is to end up with only a story, because the *classic* elements have either been deleted or diluted.

Some children like How-to-do-it or All-About Everything type books, but I suspect parents like them best because they look so educational. These really should be in a separate category because they don't usually classify as literature but are more nearly manuals of information. Paul Hazard suggests that instead of pouring out so much knowledge on a child's soul that it is crushed, we should instead plant a seed of an idea that will develop from inside. The most important knowledge is of the human heart, he concludes.

Should your child own books or just borrow them from a library? Probably some of each. Someone once said that a few well-chosen books all his own give a child a sense of value, companionship and individuality and are more valuable than fifty volumes hastily read and returned to the library. Some books, which have stood the test of time and classify as outstanding literature, should be one's own. Yet, better to buy no book than to let price dictate a poor choice. Personally I would hate to limit any child's reading experience to what he could purchase when such wonderful libraries are available. On the other hand, we can use birthdays, Christmas and special times to build a personal library.

Sometimes a parent comments, "Our older daughter loves books, but our second son seems to have no interest in reading at all."

Not all children take to books like ducks to puddles. Each child is a special person in his own way. Some are just poor readers and lack motivation. Reading comes hard for them. This is when family togetherness in books comes to the rescue, at least in part. Reading aloud and sharing a book demonstrates that stories are fun, that books are friends.

Getting them reading on their own might mean a careful curtailing of easier substitutes, but a parent in cooperation with a creative God ought to be able to come up with other assists. Try reading a very exciting story together with such a child — a story one couldn't bear to leave uncompleted — and then push the child carefully out on his own.

Make certain the project doesn't lead to failure because it is too difficult, and be available for help. Whetting his appetite this way, and then helping him find another book by the same author could mean a fresh start for the child. But it takes a sensitive parent who cares. I am convinced that many poor readers have developed psychological blocks early in their reading career, often by comparing themselves with rapid readers who leave them behind in the dust.

Don't put a premium on speed, and never say, "That book is much too young for you!" If he can read it, let him. (Make sure he doesn't have a school teacher who is belittling him this way.) Coax him onward without threatening his self-image in the complicated joy of reading.

Honey is a special treat, not a medicinal treatment.

> Happy, happy it is to be
> Where the greenwood hangs o'er the dark blue sea;
> To roam in the moonbeams clear and still
> And dance with the elves
> Over dale and hill;
> To taste their cups, and with them roam
> The fields for dewdrops and honeycomb. . . .[3]

---

[3]Walter de la Mare, *Ann and the Fairy Song.*

What Makes a Good Book

3

What Makes a Good Book

GOOD BOOKS are written not so much *for* children as written *by* people who have not lost their childhood. Since men are really only grown-up children, good books appeal to all ages. C. S. Lewis says that no book is really worth reading at the age of ten which is not equally worth reading at the age of fifty. Children's books cannot be written *for* or down *to* children. They reject books which do not treat them as equals. The "My dear little reader" approach never really pleased children.

When men first began printing books, no one thought of books for children. Only dull, moralistic books were foisted on children by adults. Hans Christian Andersen was unique in his contribution to children and his capacity for being a grown-up child. In many ways he turned the tide in children's literature, and adults were even more surprised by the way children appropriated Daniel Defoe's *Robinson Crusoe* for their very own, capturing every boy's dream of adventure.

Real books have life. They release something creative in the minds of those who absorb them. The author captures reality, the permanent stuff of life, and something is aroused in the heart of the reader that endures.

A good book has a profound kind of morality, not a cheap, sentimental sort which thrives on shallow plots and superficial heroes, but the sort of force which inspires the reader's inner life and draws out all that is noble. A good writer has something worthy to say and says it in the best possible way. Then he respects the child's ability to understand. Principles are not preached but are implicit in the writing.

Walter de la Mare says, "I know well that only the rarest kind of best in anything is good enough for the young."[1] Childhood is so brief and yet so open and formative. Impressions are taken into maturity. I cannot believe that children exposed to the best of literature will later choose that which is cheap and demeaning. That is why only the best is good enough for children, for we are shaping a future.

Of the writing of children's books today there is no end, but many of these have no claim as literature. The publishing of children's books is a profitable enterprise in our affluent society and the market is deluged with what may look on the surface to be everything a child needs. I'm not sure it is laziness that lets parents buy these; I think it is more a lack of exposure to what is truly good in children's literature.

We have already discussed simplified classics. Included in my bibliography are only two. One is *Little Pilgrim's Prog-*

---

[1]Walter de la Mare, *Bells and Grass*, Viking.

"*Mary Poppins,*" *they cried.*
"*Mary Poppins, come back!*"

ress, which in depth of writing in no way approximates the style of John Bunyan. *Pilgrim's Progress* as originally written by Bunyan is if anything more readable than the King James Bible. The marvelous imagery of this great book is couched in Bunyan's excellent prose. If you are among the families who choose the original, you will *then* have read Bunyan. But I am a realist. To miss any experience at all of the spiritual exercise and imagery of *Pilgrim's Progress* seems too great a loss to me, so I have included the simplified. The literary heart of the book is missing; but the ideas are there. Your children will be caught up in the wonder of Christian's journey and be exposed to great truths. The second is a very well-done *Tales from Shakespeare*, which hopefully will prepare the reader to enjoy Shakespeare at a later date.

The Disney-style versions of stories do children no favors. They are never as good as the original. Don't buy diluted editions. Pamela Travers *Mary Poppins* in its original form must be read if you will know Mary Poppins. And Tom Sawyer must be met in a book no matter how well the television version is received. I cajoled our son into reading Twain, and he had no embarrassment in thanking me. He remarked, "What the words help you to see and feel inside is much better than television!"

Which is precisely the problem with television; it can kill personal creativity. We don't even have to wonder what the characters look like. And while a good actor can portray intense emotion, it brings to the viewer a different experience than words do. And it cheats us out of the opportunity to learn how to express what we feel in words.

But we still haven't answered the heart of the question. What makes one book superior and another inferior? Let's begin by taking apart the elements of a book. First, we begin with the idea behind the book. What is the author trying to say? We call this the theme and a weak theme results in a flabby story.

To get across the theme, the writer must use words, language. How the author uses language is called style. Every writer forms his sentences differently and thus weaves his personality into his writing. Word choices reveal the author's skill because they carry action, emotion, truth — and make the music of good prose.

Plot is the design of the idea. Good plots grow out of strong themes. Plot doesn't answer, "What happened next?" Plot answers "Why?" The plot holds the story together in such a way that events take on meaning. Involved in plot is characterization. The skill with which the author makes the characters memorable and live for us determines in large measure the quality of the story. What a difference between the characters of Robert Louis Stevenson's *Treasure Island* and a story where the characters are like puppets on a string, enabling the reader to outguess the author. Who can forget Long John Silver, the pirate of pirates? Terrifying, yet somehow likeable; cruel, yet somehow kind; he is no stereotyped, one-handled character. If Stevenson had less artistry in defining his characters and plot, a wildly unrealistic piece of writing would have resulted and we would have long since forgotten Long John Silver.

What a convincing person Mary Poppins is! How unforgettable is Frodo of the *Hobbit* books or Toad of Toad Hall. Children can't define what charms them, but give them the right thing and they recognize it. They will have little use for stories which are shallow, insipid, awkward, labored and overly moralistic.

Letters come every day to Harper & Row addressed to Laura Ingalls Wilder, author of *Little House on the Prairie* and others. Long since dead, Laura is still alive to these children. One child wrote, "Oh, Laura, if I was you I would have kicked Nellie Oleson in the leg when she was mean to you!"

Another mother told the Harper's Children's Book editor that when they moved to a more spacious apartment with

Wilbur blushed, "But I'm not terrific,
Charlotte. I'm just average for a pig."

From *Charlotte's Web* by E. B. White, illustrated by Garth Williams. Reprinted with permission of Harper and Row, Publishers.

a guest room, her son had asked eagerly, "Now can Mr. White come and stay overnight with us?" He loved the author because he had given him the joy of *Charlotte's Web*. A young friend of ours sent one of her stories to C. S. Lewis asking for his critique and inquiring into his method for plotting stories. Because he is C. S. Lewis, he answered her as seriously as he would have answered a letter from an important man of letters. Children *do* know. Only this summer, a ten-year old sighed. "I wish Mr. Lewis had not died. I'd like more of his kind of stories."

The quality of the idea, the skill of the plot, the depth of characterization, the distinctive style of the author — that's the best I can do by way of defining a good book.

No one has yet sat down and devised a set of rules that magically produces a great story. The quality that we have talked about has to come from the quality inside the person writing the story. In 1945 Jesse Jackson wrote *Call Me Charley*, the story of the only black boy in a white school. Mr. Jackson did not set out to deliver a message on race relations. He simply wrote a book out of his own experience. It had the ring of reality, and twenty years later the book's editor would hear a woman tell how she had read a book in the fifth grade that changed her life, her whole attitude about people. The book was *Call Me Charley*.

What is excellent has a certain spirit of literature present. The sensitivity of the reader says, "This is true." "This is real." And it sets in action something in the reader which profoundly affects him. It has been an experience — spiritual, imaginative, intellectual or social. A sense of permanent worthwhileness surrounds really great literature. Laughter, pain, hunger, satisfaction, love, joy — the ingredients of human life are found in depth and leave a residue of mental and spiritual richness in the reader.

If we familiarize our children with this kind of writing, then they have a ground for making comparisons. Not everything they read will be excellent, but they will know a story's possibilities. It will set their reading patterns in motion.

I have already mentioned the importance of illustrations. A great variety of styles should be part of a child's inheritance, not just the parent's current preference. Bright colors, gentle pastels, bold strokes, whimsical lines, quaint old-fashioned pictures, modern design, pen and ink sketches — the story will demand a certain mood for the child. Some of you may not like the illustrators I have noted, but over the years children have chosen them as favorites.

Some books simply look more readable than others. White space, style of type and paper quality may decide what is acceptable. That is to say, a good book should look like a good book!

Have you ever noticed children look for a book in the library? They stare at the bindings, reading the titles. So many books, so many shelves — how does one choose? A few children whose parents have taught them which authors to look for or how to choose a book may invade the library with the confidence of a vacuum cleaner, scooping up everything good in sight. But for most this is not true. Parents know what I mean, because without some help, they feel a similar bewilderment. The librarian is often otherwise involved and not available for help. I know so well the anguish of a child who asks, "Teacher, could you help me find a good book?" Knowing about good books requires some learning time.

That's why I have written this book. The bibliography does not contain *all* the good books available, but it is a beginning. These have stood the test of time and/or of children's choice. Notice authors' names and teach your children to do likewise. It's the secret to capturing library-fear. If your child enjoys one of Kate Seredy's books (and I hope she does!) then she will doubtless want to read others by this author. Experience is the best teacher.

Don't make the mistake of saying, "Here is a book you must read." A child may decide without opening the cover that this is just the book he does *not* want to read. Don't force any book. Make excursions to the library a learning time for you and the children. Better to say, "This book looks like fun."

or "Here's one you might enjoy."

or "What do you think of this book?"

In our family we recommend books to each other regularly and take opinions seriously. It's lonely not to have someone else share a book which has touched you in some way. Family closeness is not suddenly developed when children reach a certain age; it must begin from the first. A special joy comes when you hear your small child say to you, "You'll love it," as he recommends Lois Lenski's *Little Train*.

One of my favorite memories involves just such a time of sharing a book. Traveling abroad we had purchased Elizabeth Goudge's *The Little White Horse* for our twelve-year-old son to read. He enjoyed it so much he repeatedly said, "Mom, you've just got to read this book." One night I stayed back from an art lecture in Florence, Italy, that I had hoped to attend, and spent the evening with him instead. I read *that* book. I was as delighted as he, and commented on incidents as I read on. He was absorbed in his own book, but suddenly came over to my chair, gave me a tight hug and said spontaneously, "I just had to tell you this minute I loved you!" I was taking time to enjoy *his* book. I treasure that evening. No art lecture could have done for us what sharing that book did, and later Father read it aloud to us again.

One of the teachers in our city read Roald Dahl's *Charlie and the Chocolate Factory* to her class. They must have shared the fun of the book on the playground because seemingly half of the school came into the library to ask for the book. The librarian got the idea finally and ordered several copies. She said to me, "It isn't on *any* list, but I can't keep a copy on the shelves." Which all goes to show that children will like what they will and I suspect that's how books get on lists.

Every child in your family may not like every book in this bibliography. That would be expecting far too much. You may ask, "Why didn't she put this book on her list? We loved it." There wasn't room for them all. Keep it on your list and share the title with others. The bibliography has this caption, *Books Children Should Have the Opportunity to Enjoy*. Expose them to the variety, read some of the books aloud, but let the children ultimately decide what they enjoy.

You will notice some books are labelled Caldecott or New-berry Award winners. Librarians tell me that some parents come in and without any reference to the child's interest ask, "I'd like a Caldecott book." The 1967 Newberry Award winner illustrates the folly of this. Irene Hunt's *Up a Road Slowly* is a beautifully written story for a teenage girl who is by nature reflective and serious. Saying, "This is good litera-ture" will probably not make a carefree tomboy like it. Wis-dom demands that as parents we make some effort to under-stand both books and children.

Boys and girls go through a stage, usually around ten years of age, where they consume series books. Christian and secular publishers have numerous adventure series. For some it will be *Sugar Creek Gang* books; for others it will be the *Tarzan* series. *The Twin series* by Lucy Fitch Perkins are also quite popular. None in my bibliography fall into this classification, but that is not because they are harmful. In general, they just do not classify as superior literature but seem to meet a need in a child's life. While waiting for this stage to pass, I'd be ready to recommend some others at the right moment.

Good literature teaches more than we know. Example al-ways speaks louder than precept, and books can do more to inspire honor and tenacity of purpose than all the scoldings and exhortations in the world.

The teaching is accumulative, too. The other day our high schooler was discussing two destructive children. He said, "I got to thinking about how I would teach my children not to pull up wild flowers by the roots and destroy things, and then I wondered how I had learned myself. I decided I had learned from books to respect the world. In C. S. Lewis books the animals and trees have personality; in pioneer stories Indians tried to walk through the forest without breaking a twig and settlers respected the land; in Tolkien's books, the orcs are the bad guys who leave a path of careless destruction." He concluded, "You put a whole childhood of reading together and you don't have to take a conservation course."

Poetry

4

Poetry

What is Poetry? Who knows?
Not the rose, but the scent of the rose;
Not the sky, but the light in the sky;
Not the fly, but the gleam of the fly;
Not the sea, but the sound of the sea;
Not myself, but what makes me
See, hear and feel something that prose
Cannot: and what it is, who knows![1]

POETRY IS A KIND of verbal music. It is more than just doggerel that rhymes. It appeals more to feelings than to intellect. In poetry we get the shape and feel of words. Chil-

---

[1] Eleanor Farjeon, *Poems for Children*, Lippincott.

dren may learn to appreciate poetry more than adults because they are free to let it be what it is and not demand more of it.

Children first meet poetry in the repetitious rhythm of nursery rhymes. Most of them are nonsensical . . .

"A pocketful of rye, four and twenty blackbirds baked in a pie . . ." (What a feathery idea!)

"Jack and Jill went up the hill to fetch a pail of water . . ." (Strange place to find a well!)

But the sense really doesn't matter. In fact, I must confess that some poems which come most frequently to my mind are nonsensical ones from happy childhood memories. Their beat and verbal song seem to stick. That's why children often say when hearing nursery rhymes read, "Sing it again."

I have in my notebook an interesting quote that bears on the subject. Whether it came from a conversation or a famous writer, I have long since forgotten, but it is worth sharing. "Do you know what is wrong with people who never read nursery rhymes? I will tell you. When little boys and girls grow bigger and older, they should grow from the outside, leaving a little boy in the middle; even when they are quite grown up, the little child that once they were should be within them. But some unlucky people grow older from inside and so grow old through and through." That has always seemed a dreadful fate to me.

The first poetry books used at our house included Milne's *When We Were Very Young* and *Now We Are Six*. The poems vary from the nonsensical and eccentric to the warm and familiar. The contribution of Ernest Shepard's excellent illustrations add much to our enjoyment of these poems. Here are some excerpts:

> They're changing the guard at Buckingham Palace —
> Christopher Robin went down with Alice.
> Alice is marrying one of the guard,
> "A soldier's life is terrible hard,"
>
> Says Alice.

Ring-o ring o'roses.

From *Book of Nursery and Mother Goose Rhymes* by Marguerite di Angeli. Copyright 1953, 1954 by Marguerite di Angeli. Reprinted by permission of Doubleday & Company, Inc.

or,

> Ernest was an elephant, a great big fellow
> Leonard was a lion with a six foot tail,
> George was a goat, and his beard was yellow,
> And James was a very small snail.

From an appealing cadence such as this, what would you naturally name a lion or a goat at your house?

Have you ever loved to chant this one while taking a walk?

> Whenever I walk in a London street,
> I'm ever so careful to watch my feet,
>   And I keep in the squares
>   And the masses of bears
> Who wait at the corners all ready to eat
> The sillies who tread on the lines of the street,
>   Go back to their lairs
>   And I say to them, "Bears,
> Just look how I'm walking in all of the squares!"[2]

By all means give children generous doses of A. A. Milne, Edward Lear and Hilaire Belloc — just for fun.

Reading poetry is not the same as reading a story. Listening to poetry, a child becomes accustomed to words in an unfamiliar arrangement, and to the cadence of the meter. Words "rise and fall and flow and pause and echo — like the singing of birds at daybreak or a little before the fall of night when daffodils 'take the winds of March with beauty'."[3]

Poetry is like music in that it has to have sound to be appreciated. Reading poetry aloud to a receptive child is one of the rewards of parenthood. The surprise and beauty of

---

[2]A. A. Milne, *When We Were Very Young*, Dutton.
[3]Walter de la Mare, *Tom Tiddler's Ground*, Knopf.

There was an Old Man on
  whose nose
Most birds of the
  air could repose;
But they all flew away at the closing of day,
Which relieved that Old Man and his nose.

From *The Complete Nonsense Book* by Edward Lear. Reprinted
with permission of Dodd, Mead & Company.

words may break on a child like the dawning of a fresh world and he will be forever a lover of poetry.

Poems, like good seasonings, should be sprinkled lightly on the life of a child. One here, another delightful one there. Too much deadens the ability to hear and helps some children decide that poetry is wearisome. Boys and girls usually have a natural ear for poetry and a great capacity for enjoyment if the development of this kind of reading keeps pace with growth in other areas.

Lewis Gannett, who compiled *The Family Book of Verse*, writes, "When I was small, my father read poetry to the family at breakfast each morning, and on Sunday afternoons he read longer poetry to those who came to listen. I seem to recall sometimes resenting the morning delay before eating . . . yet, rereading old poems . . . again and again I seem to be hearing — and appreciating — echoes of my father's voice. I observe that my daughter reads every night — sometimes poetry — to her six daughters and they obviously enjoy it. It would be a proud boast if this book should help encourage the old custom of reading poetry aloud at home."

I include Gannett's comments for obvious reasons. Your children may not coax you to read a poem. Sometimes when you are bent upon sharing one, they may give you a look of patient endurance. But valuable experiences are not always appreciated at the time; later they yield their rewards. We do many things for our families because we decide they are *right* to do. The spirit, the attitude, the sense of adventure with which they are done makes all the difference! And I have often seen in our house a warm look of love that says secretly, "My father is special!" when my husband reads a poem, introducing it with, "My Dad used to read this to us. . . ."

Of course, you'll want to hear some from Robert Louis Stevenson's *A Child's Garden of Verses* for warmth of child-

I wonder . . . why
God put the sky
So high. . . .

From *I Wonder Why* by Joan Summer. Used by permission of
Moody Press.

hood pleasures. My mother used to waken us in the morning
with this one:

> A birdie with a yellow bill
> Hopped upon the window sill.
> Cocked his shining eye and said,
> "Ain't you 'shamed, you sleepy-head?"

or do you remember

> I saw you toss the kites on high
> And blow the birds about the sky;
> And all around I heard you pass
> Like ladies' skirts across the grass —
> O wind, a-blowing all day long,
> O wind, that sings so loud a song![4]

Eleanor Farjeon's poetry for children has a wit and melody all its own. Sounds and senses are accentuated in the poetry of Carl Sandburg and Robert Frost. Here is Frost's
The Pasture:

> I'm going out to clean the pasture spring;
> I'll only stop to rake the leaves away
> (And wait to watch the water clear, I may):
> I sha'n't be gone long — You come too.
>
> I'm going out to fetch the little calf
> That's standing by the mother. It's so young,
> It totters when she licks it with her tongue.
> I sha'n't be gone long — You come too.[5]

Feel Carl Sandburg's *Fog*:

> The fog comes
> on little cat feet.
> It sits looking

---

[4]Robert L. Stevenson, *A Child's Garden of Verses*, Scribner.
[5]Robert Frost, *You Come Too*, Holt.

I wonder . . . why at night
When I climb into my bed,
I always feel so extra good
After my prayers are said. . . .

From *I Wonder Why* by Joan Summer. Used by permission of
Moody Press.

> over harbor and city
> on silent haunches
> and then moves on.[6]

Sara Teasdale and Christina Rossetti often write about nature. Children feel in their hearts what Sara Teasdale shares in this excerpt from *Barter*:

> Life has loveliness to sell —
> All beautiful and splendid things,
> Blue waves whitened on a cliff,
> Climbing fire that sways and sings,
> And children's faces looking up
> Holding wonder like a cup.[7]

Each poet brings his own style, his own emotional wealth to the poem. Anthologies give us the best opportunity to sample many flavors of poetry. Several of these are listed in the bibliography.

When you are first introducing poetry to a child you will use happy verse — nonsensical, exaggerated, cozy — whatever you choose. As the child grows older, don't shy away from poetry which you may think is too deep or too sad for him. Trust the child to understand more than he can express. He may or may not say to you, "That poem understands me," but that may be what he feels inside. For instance, listen to the mood of Edna St. Vincent Millay's *God's World*:

> O world, I cannot hold thee close enough!
> Thy winds, thy wide gray skies!
> Thy mists that roll and rise!
> Thy woods, this autumn day, that ache and sag
> And all but cry with color! . . .[8]

---

[6]*The Family Book of Verse*, ed. L. Gannett, Harper.
[7]*Ibid.*
[8]*Ibid.*

or Emily Dickinson's *Have You Got a Brook?*

> Have you got a brook in your little heart,
> Where bashful flowers blow,
> And blushing birds go down to drink
> And shadows tremble so?
>
> And nobody knows, so still it flows,
> That any brook is there;
> And yet your little draught of life
> Is daily drunken there. . . .[9]

By all means, share old favorites like Longfellow's *Paul Revere's Ride;*

> Listen, my children, and you shall hear
> Of the midnight ride of Paul Revere,
> On the eighteenth of April, in Seventy-five;
> Hardly a man is now alive
> Who remembers that famous day and year. . . .[10]

or the romance of Alfred Noyes' *The Highwayman*:

> The wind was a torrent of darkness among the gusty trees,
> The moon was a ghostly galleon tossed upon cloudy seas,
> The road was a ribbon of moonlight over the purple moor,
>   And the highwayman came riding —
>   Riding — riding —
> The highwayman came riding, up to the old inn door. . . .[11]

Samuel Taylor Coleridge's *The Rime of the Ancient Mariner* will stir the heart of a child who is turning to his teens. Don't you remember the thirsty feeling of this haunting tale?

> Water, water everywhere,
> And all the boards did shrink;

---

[9]*Ibid.*
[10]*Ibid.*
[11]*Ibid.*

> Water, water everywhere,
> Nor any drop to drink.[12]

Or read his *Christobel* and *Kubla Khan*, so rich in imagination. The list extends endlessly, for there are so many to be met and enjoyed — William Blake, E. E. Cummings, John Donne, Kipling and others.

Do you remember hearing *Sea Fever?*

> I must down to the seas again, to the lonely sea and the sky,
> And all I ask is a tall ship and a star to steer her by.[13]

This song of the sea was written by John Masefield who also penned a magnificent Christian poem, *The Everlasting Mercy*, one you will want to share with your older children.

One can hardly forget Francis Thompson's *The Hound of Heaven*, portraying so vividly man's flight from God:

> I fled Him, down the nights and down the days;
> I fled Him, down the arches of the years . . .[14]

It's a great spiritual experience to share with your children. But long before they are old enough to understand the fascinating account of *The Hound of Heaven*, they ought to meet Francis Thompson in *Ex Ore Infantium*, one of my favorites:

> Little Jesus, wast Thou shy
> Once, and just so small as I?
> And what did it feel like to be
> Out of heaven, and just like me? . . .[15]

Ernest Thayer's *Casey at the Bat* or Robert Service's *The Cremation of Sam McGee* will capture the imagination of

---

[12]*Ibid.*
[13]*Ibid.*
[14]*Ibid.*
[15]*Ibid.*

some who will have none of the mystical imagery of other
verse. Explore, take time out to browse through good anthologies for children and find some new joys for yourself
as well.

The *Psalms* are rich in poetic melody.

> He who dwells in the shelter of the Most High,
> Who abides in the Shadow of the Almighty,
> Will say to the Lord, "My refuge and my fortress;
> My God, in whom I trust."[16]

After you've read about the Red Sea incident, enjoy that
wonderful song of Moses,

> I will sing unto the Lord,
>   for he has triumphed gloriously;
> The horse and his rider
>   he has thrown into the sea.[17]

When reading of David's sin with Bathsheba, include
Psalm 51,

> Have mercy on me, O God,
> According to Thy steadfast love;
> According to Thy abundant mercy
>   blot out my transgressions.

Or the prayer of Moses, the man of God, in Psalm 90.
Picture old Moses, leading the children of Israel, and listen,

> Lord, Thou hast been our dwelling place
>   in all generations.
> Before the mountains were brought forth,
> Or ever Thou hadst formed the earth and the world,
> From everlasting to everlasting Thou art God.

---

[16]Psalm 91:1.
[17]Exodus 15:1.

Jeremiah captures mankind's perpetual wandering:

> For my people have committed two evils:
>   they have forsaken me,
> The fountain of living waters,
>   and hewed out cisterns for themselves,
>   broken cisterns
>   that can hold no water.[18]

You will notice I have stuck closely to old favorites in this chapter on poetry, but that is not without purpose. They *are* favorites because people have loved them, and this is a good place to begin. Their lines sing and their content is not obscure. As you move on into the world of poetry, you will find unfamiliar meter, blank verse, an irregular kind of prose called poetry. Don't be afraid to try it out for size; it may fit your mood very well.

If you share poetry with your children, someday you will know the delight of their sharing favorites with you. I picked up our ninth grader one afternoon at school to take him to the barbershop for a haircut. He reached into his back pocket and drew out a sheet of notebook paper, folded many times, saying, "We studied this in school today and I thought you'd like it." While he was getting his hair cut, I sat in the car and read what he had bothered to copy for my enjoyment:

> They are the Slaves who fear to speak
> For the fallen and the weak;
> They are the slaves who will not choose
> Hatred, scoffing and abuse,
> Rather than in silence shrink
> From the truth they needs must think;
> They are the slaves who dare not be
> In the right with two or three.[19]

Sharing makes for lovely companionship.

---

[18] Jeremiah 2:13.
[19] James Russell Lowell, *They Are the Slaves.*

The Pleasure of a Shared Adventure

5

The Pleasure of a Shared Adventure

"IF FAMILIES don't read books together, how do they know each other's friends?"

That's exactly how we feel about it.

Reading aloud as a family has bound us together, as sharing an adventure always does. We *do* know the same people. We have gone through emotional crises together as we felt anger, sadness, fear, gladness and tenderness in the world of the book we are reading. Something happens to us which is better experienced than described — a kind of enlarging of heart — when we encounter passages full of grand language and nobility of thought.

Much of our secret family idiom comes from the books we have read together. I say "secret" because a specialness surrounds it. You need to have shared the book to know what the phrase means, and when we use it, it's communication with the heart.

Sometimes it is silly doggerel like Horton's declaration of faithfulness in Dr. Seuss' *Horton Hatches an Egg*:

> I meant what I said
> And I said what I meant,
> An elephant is faithful
> One hundred percent.

Other times we speak of *Narnian air, the Ents, Barkis is willin', a useful pot for putting things in,* and hundreds of like phrases. When we went to visit a favorite spot and saw that much of what we remembered as beautiful had changed, our son said, "The orcs have been here," and we didn't need to say more.

We don't read a book to get a family vocabulary, you understand. It is just a cozy by-product worth mentioning only because of the intimacy of experience it expresses. That's the important part.

Not infrequently parents complain of inability to communicate with their children. "I cannot understand how he thinks!" I want to ask if they ever *really* thought together about ideas. Parents may treat children as *children* most of their lives — giving them "milk," working hard to provide opportunities for them — and then suddenly the children are on the verge of adulthood and they have never become acquainted with them as *people*. It *is* frightening to suddenly find people living in your household whom you don't know!

You can't one day decide to *know* your children and have it magically happen. You begin from the beginning by sharing "the honey" of life, as well as providing "the milk." Knowing someone means sharing ideas, growing together. It means not being embarrassed about feelings or being yourself.

As a small boy our son frequently commented, "I like him. He treats me like I'm a people." It's become a family joke, but being treated like "a people" means being taken seriously and being liked for who you really are. Interpersonal relationships within a family develop on this level.

At the age of seventy Laurence Housman writes about the contribution reading made in his family in *The Unexpected Years*, "These family readings formed so satisfying a bond between older and younger that I can hardly think of family life without it; and I marvel when I hear of families in whose upbringing it has had no place."

In this day of committees and television, we don't marvel as Mr. Housman does, but we do recommend family reading with great enthusiasm for we have seen what it has done for our family and the immense pleasure and richness it has brought. Finishing the last book of Tolkien's trilogy was some of the most exciting reading we've ever done. A recent trip by car across the state was especially "delicious" because we were able to get extra chapters read as we drove along together. We share Mr. Housman's sentiments.

Family reading aloud *demands* good literature. Only the best can stand the test of hearing the words hit the airwaves and falling into the minds of such a variety of ages. You won't find a busy father reading insipid, sentimental stories aloud for very long — and the best family reading requires a father's voice. (That's a fact, however, not an excuse. Our father's work demanded that he travel, sometimes as much as fifty per cent of the time. We kept a special book we only read when he was home, and another which we read when he was gone. But we always felt compelled to give him great, long summaries of what we were reading so he wouldn't feel left out!)

At the outset, with child number one, begin with the simple but good stories that were favorites in your own childhood or that you've recently discovered. While the plot may not hold you as adults, something about it seems to come alive with freshness and gives what someone described as "a spring time urge to make them more beguiling than they ever sounded before."

Soon stories move into quite another class because children can understand far more than is sometimes guessed. When child number two comes along and is big enough to join the reading circle, if the favorites have been special literature they bear repeating and no one minds. Each child deserves some catching up along the way, but do keep moving on up.

A family of four, ages five to twelve, read aloud together with the two older children in mind. The youngest, even if she doesn't always understand, feels the comfortable security of Father's voice and of being included in the "inner circle." Sometimes she falls asleep in his arms, but she would rather be there with the family than in bed alone. Not infrequently the older children take special pleasure in re-reading past favorites with the younger ones, and that's a good kind of sharing, too.

"A book read aloud is a book better remembered, especially if the reading took place in childhood," writes William Henry Chamberlain in *Saturday Review*. "One of the first books my father read to me was that old, romantic war horse, *Ivanhoe*, by Sir Walter Scott. It has been decades since I last picked it up; but my memory, even for quite trivial incidents, is still quite keen. I can almost reconstruct from memory the language of the scene where a haughty Norman baron exclaims derogatorily, 'Your Highness may call me a Saxon!' to receive a prompt rebuff from stout old Cedric, the father of Ivanhoe, 'Who calls thee a Saxon will do thee an honor as great as it is undeserved.'"

Reading aloud doesn't allow anyone to set a speed record, but this is one of its advantages. How nice to amble together through the descriptive paragraphs which might otherwise be raced past, and take a leisurely look around. One sees and feels more this way.

Characters seem more real when a story is read with some gift of expression. Maybe it is because a whole family is identifying with the characters and this strengthens the bonds one feels. Beautiful writing is seen more clearly to be what it is. We often interject, "That is magnificent!" or "What terrific insight!" And sometimes the reader gets a lump so large in his throat over the beauty or pathos of a situation that we all pause to swallow back our agony before going on. Who can read of Sidney Carton's vision of the future before he goes off to the guillotine in *A Tale of Two Cities* without a tear? Or of Aslan's marvelous reappearance after being killed in *The Lion, The Witch and The Wardrobe* without emotion?

I've already mentioned some of our favorite read-aloud books, but don't let these suggestions keep you from discovering others. We've read and re-read *Winnie the Pooh* more times than anyone would believe. Pooh books have a kind of wisdom and humor that gets better with the years. All of his friends are like people we know. As Poohphiles we play Pooh Sticks on the bridge, we've gone on many an expotition to the North Pole, and we have wished to unbounce many a Tigger. It's annoying to see A. A. Milne's classic listed under a five-to-nine age bracket. Pooh is a collegiate favorite!

The Jungle Doctor series by Paul White of Australia have made good family reading. Dr. White is a superb storyteller in African fashion, and his stories excite both children and adults. As a modern day Aesop, his *Monkey Tales* and *Jungle Doctor's Fables* speak a worldwide language, using the enchantment of animals to teach deeper lessons. Since he was formerly a missionary doctor, Paul White's stories are set in Tanzania and reflect the missionary and his message.

Patricia St. John's books have been read aloud at appropriate ages in our family. Our favorites were *Treasures of*

The goat who wanted to become a lion.

the Snow (a Swiss setting) and *Star of Light*, which is a touching story of an unwanted girl in a Muslim home in Morocco and of her courageous brother.

Topping our list of best-reading are the seven children's books of C. S. Lewis — the Narnia books, we call them. These seven gems have delighted us numerous times, each fresh reading providing new insights. What makes them so special? Excellent weaving of plot and characters into a most exciting, imaginative series of adventures, with the masterful skill of C. S. Lewis' style. But even more than this: the quality of the idea behind the stories!

The Narnia books are allegories and, as such, are rich in Christian thought. Profoundly Christian, the father in our house would say. Apart from the allegory, the books stand as superbly written adventure stories, and schoolteachers have held their classes spellbound with them without ever alluding to the allegory. Yet it is the allegory which has added the plus of pleasure for our family.

We began reading *The Lion, the Witch and the Wardrobe*, never mentioning what we as parents saw in the White Witch or in Aslan, the golden-maned Lion. Four children enter this magical land of Narnia which is under the rule of the White Witch — a land where it is always winter and never gets to Christmas. That is, until Aslan comes and brings Spring and hope again. The children see Aslan captured by the witch, shorn of his majestic mane, tormented and finally killed. We ached with the four children in their sadness, and then suddenly on the third day, Aslan is alive and comes bounding over the hill. At this point our seven-year-old couldn't get the words out fast enough in his excitement, "He's like the Lord Jesus. Aslan *is* the Lord Jesus!" What a wonderful moment. Aslan, the golden-maned Lion of the Tribe of Judah!

Each time we finished one book we were sure the next in the series couldn't be as good. When we read *The Last Battle* we felt we had been introduced to the most creative thinking

Illustration by Ernest H. Shepard (copyright 1933 Charles Scribner's Sons, renewal copyright © 1961 Ernest H. Shepard) reproduced with the permission of Charles Scribner's Sons from *The Wind in the Willows*, page 92, by Kenneth Grahame.

about heaven we had ever done. Shortly after reading this, a neighbor boy, who had stayed overnight and thus been exposed to our family Bible reading at the breakfast table, commented, "I don't think I want to go to heaven. Who wants to sit around all day? I want to do something." What fun we had hearing our eight-year-old tell him that heaven wasn't going to be like that. Why, you could run with a unicorn and never get tired; you could even run up a waterfall, and the further in you got the better life tasted! If this sounds insane to you, then you'll have to read the book, and I hope you do.

The Wind in the Willows by Kenneth Grahame has been loved by children and adults for sixty years. Sometime around your child's eighth birthday, you ought to read it aloud together. The fellowship of Rat and Mole and Mr. Toad is too good to miss. Here again is an enduring quality of writing, rich in feeling and the author's commitment to the world he creates. When Ernest Shepard illustrated the story, he visited Kenneth Grahame in England, walking along the river bank to make sketches of the setting for the story. "I love these little people," said Grahame, "be kind to them. Make them real." And they do become real as you meet in the story, and their sayings will surely become part of your family idioms. Who can forget the Christmas scene at Mole End, with the little mice, red mufflers wrapped around their throats, standing in a semi-circle outside, singing,

> Villagers all, this frosty tide
> Let your doors swing open wide.

The list of good read-aloud books is too long to continue carrying on in such detail, but I must mention some others.

C. S. Lewis was profoundly influenced by George MacDonald. *The Princess and the Goblin* and others by MacDonald have the same kind of supernatural touch. As one young girl said, "I like these books the way I like the Narnia ones." Rich in wisdom, these books are some your children should investigate.

Alice in Wonderland, Charlotte's Web, Mary Poppins, Dr. Dolittle, The Jungle Books — I hope you won't miss any of these.

At about eleven years of age, or perhaps a little older, we went on to *David Copperfield, Oliver Twist,* and eventually *A Tale of Two Cities.* Charles Dickens' characters are magnificent; we *know* Wilkins Micawber, Lil' Emily, Peggotty, Uriah Heep, Oliver and all the others. We didn't discuss these books as classics; we simply read them and enjoyed them.

At one point we read the unabridged edition of *Robinson Crusoe* together. My husband's freshmen poetry teacher sent it to Mark as a gift, but it became a gift for my husband and me as well, because we had never read this as Defoe wrote it. We were outraged that a condensation had cheated us out of so much — even the seemingly dreary passages which describe the hopelessness of his future on the island. Then one day Crusoe discovered a Bible in the bottom of an old trunk and we saw the man we had known only as a shipwrecked victim become a believer in Jesus Christ. No child listening to this story could miss the convincing difference his conversion made in Crusoe's view of the island and life.

But do be wise in your choice of books. Don't force your children to appreciate any of these books. There are too many other good books to choose from which may meet their needs and yours more fully. Reading should be fun.

Reading J. R. R. Tolkien's *The Hobbit* and *The Lord of the Rings* has been an experience. Here is a masterful spinner of tales! We are awed by the power of language, the depth of characterization, the force of the adventure. The test of good writing is the quality of the experience we receive in reading it. This is great writing! By all means, read Tolkien.

We finished the last book of the Tolkien trilogy, *The Return of the King,* on a wilderness canoe trip in the Canadian bush last summer. One morning when the wind was cold and strong, we huddled together in the largest tent to read. We were at such an exciting point in the book, it was easy to go on for several chapters. The tale was reaching its climax, the reader was having difficulty with the lump in his throat, and all of us had wet eyes over the sheer beauty of the scene of triumph after the destruction of the evil ring. If you haven't read the book, can you still feel with us the fulfillment of victory, of utter joy as the King comes into his own rightful place and all his warriors are honored?

> And all the host laughed and wept, and in the midst of their merriment and tears the clear voice of the minstrel rose like silver and gold, and all men were hushed. And he sang to them, now in the Elven-tongue, now in the speech of the West, until their hearts, wounded with sweet words, overflowed, and their joy was like swords, and they passed in thought out to regions where pain and delight flow together and tears are the very wine of blessedness.[1]

Later, when we prayed together by a moonlit shore, a seventeen-year-old thanked God not just for "beautiful things we can see, but for beautiful words which remind us of realities we cannot see."

While we have been tingling with excitement over these lengthy stories, I have thought repeatedly of Paul Hazard's words about "books that awaken in them (the readers) not maudlin sentimentality, but sensibility; that enable them to share in great human emotion; that give them respect for universal life — that of animals, of plants; that teach them not to despise everything that is mysterious in creation and in men."[2]

---

[1] J.R.R. Tolkien, *The Return of the King,* Ballantine, p. 286.
[2] Paul Hazard, *Books, Children and Men,* Horn Books.

I have mentioned two of the by-products of reading aloud: family closeness because of a shared experience, and the bond of appreciation of good writing. The third factor has been alluded to: the opportunity of teaching what is true and good.

Cruelty, evil, greed come into clear focus against kindness, truth and honor in a well-written story. (I say *well-written* because nothing offends a child more than having to be told when something is mean and base or noble and good. This painful spelling out of what one is supposed to learn from a story evidences the author's inability to create valid characters in a real life plot. And it insults children.)

The best teaching we have done in our family has been through reading the Bible and good books aloud together. It is really not such a profound concept. How would you best be enlightened to some truth — by being told that it was wrong to be nasty and thoughtless to others, or to meet and come to love some character in a story and then feel her hurts when someone is unkind and says cruel things?

We sometimes talk about the characters we meet in our stories and about the motivation of their deeds. We discuss worthy ideas and try to hang important concepts into a larger framework of truth. The Christian parent who uses both the Book and books has a distinct advantage. The Bible spells out the precepts, the teaching of God's plan for man. It also tells us about real people — their faith, their sins, their courage, their disbelief — and we see the fruit of each in what follows in their lives. Good books fulfill our human need for adventure and wider experience, but they also provide support for the kind of character development of which the Scriptures speak.

When we meet a situation in a story where there is trouble and no faith, a child may say spontaneously, "Oh, if he only knew that God could help him!" Reading *The Adventures of Robin Hood* we discussed some pretty important issues when a tearful child asked, "Did Robin Hood go to heaven? He was such a good man." We didn't completely solve our mutual sorrow over Robin's death in the story, but some weightier matters were touched upon.

But deeper than this have been those elements of great strength of character and largeness of heart that I have spoken of earlier. These are intangible things. One cannot drive a point home and say, "There he has learned that lesson." But by continual exposure to a variety of people and experiences, the real values of life are taught most profoundly.

Again, I recall a quote of Paul Hazard, "I like books that set in action truths worthy of lasting forever, and of inspiring one's whole inner life. . . ."[3]

What a pleasure to share that kind of a book with a child!

[3]Paul Hazard, *Books, Children and Men*, Horn Books.

Honey From the Rock

6

Honey From the Rock

MY GRANDFATHER was a Dutch immigrant with ten children. He and Grandmother took seriously the instructions given by God in Deuteronomy 6, believing this to be a Christian parent's responsibility:

These words which I command you this day shall be upon your heart; and you shall teach them diligently to your children, and shall talk of them when you sit in your house, and when you walk by the way and when you lie down, and when you rise.

As the family gathered around the table for meals, one of my grandparents read from the Bible, usually three times a day. It was a kind of spiritual dessert. They had enjoyed physical food from the hand of God; now they would enjoy spiritual food.

My father was one of these children. Later, when four small offspring sat around his table, he initiated the same practice. (As far as I know, his brothers and sisters have done similarly in their homes.) We never discussed whether or not we wanted to do this; it was just always done and never, to my knowledge, questioned. Reading material was chosen according to our ages. Often at the evening meal we read from a Bible story book, but at least once a day we read short selections from the Bible. For some reason we read *Proverbs* more than any other single book; my parents must have believed that book contained an extraordinary amount of wisdom for everyday living.

To the children in our family this was a logical thing for a Christian family to do. No one left the table, unless for special reasons, until we read the Scriptures together. This was no legalistic ritual; it was family habit. Thinking back, I remember numerous instances in which our friends called for us and we asked them to wait until we had finished dinner. Dessert may have been served, but none of us ever considered the meal finished until we had read together.

As I recounted this to a group of young couples recently, one father asked me, "Didn't you all grow up resenting your father and Christianity?" I felt an aching kind of amusement at his question.

"Quite the other way around," I answered. In all honesty, our parents and memories of family life are *extra* dear because of this. Four new families have come out of our parental home, involving fourteen children from four years to twenty-two, and each family follows the pattern we learned at home. Our expectations are that each of these fourteen will pursue a similar practice in their homes in years to come.

I laugh when I visit my brothers' homes and hear them stop in the middle of the reading to ask a child they suspect is not listening, "David, what was the last word?" That's what my father used to do. It will be fun to see if the grandsons use the same device.

Why is it that family Bible reading is such a rare thing in today's Christian homes, especially when it is the most alive, pertinent book in the world? Why did that young father expect that disciplined Scripture reading would produce resentment? Let me suggest several reasons.

1. Too many have a phony image of what this involves. Their minds conjure up pictures of a "family altar" with a large open Bible on the table against a background of flowers or a picture of Jesus. Around this scene, the family is piously kneeling for a minor church service each night. The people seem unreal, the language is that of Zion, and the experience looks as painful as possible.

But that image is a pretty shabby excuse for not making the Word of God central in our homes. Shouting about all of the abuses of the practice is hardly a creative exercise and it doesn't fool God for one minute. We need less reactions and a good deal more action if our homes are going to stand the test of an increasingly secular world.

2. Parents are not really convinced of the importance of biblical instruction. *Not really*, I said. Because we do arrange for what we believe is important. Life is never so busy that we don't manage to see that our family has nourishing food, adequate clothing and proper sleep. And, yes, we see that they get to Sunday school, church, youth organizations and all the busy extras of life.

But parents who never themselves read God's Word outside of an organized meeting of the church are not likely to sense the urgency of instructing children in the most important Truth in the world. If we really believe that knowing God and His Son is the most vital experience in the world, how dare we leave the responsibility for instruction to someone else?

3. Parents lack the discipline that makes family life work. Parents need to live their lives with conviction, not hesitatingly. If you must make a fresh decision each day *whether* you will read the Scriptures and *when* you will read them, the Scriptures will probably not be read very often. Increasingly, Christian family life has little to distinguish it from secular family life.

Eating together, giving thanks for daily mercies should be a basic feature of our home life. In a discussion-growth group someone asked, "What was your favorite room in your family home?" I said without hesitation, "The breakfast room." That is where we ate our meals and were all together. We talked about the day, about our burning ideas and shared our new jokes. Often one of our parents had to keep order by giving permission to speak because we all wanted to talk at once. No one left the table as soon as he had finished his food. Of course, I've already said that we read briefly at the close of the meal, but leaving would also mean that I didn't care what my brother was planning to do or what happened in my sister's day, an unthinkable lack of courtesy. Naturally we were nasty to each other on occasions, but this didn't change our family pattern.

I suppose there is nothing sacred about eating together in one sense, yet isn't it strange how important this was when believers met together in the New Testament? And just exactly where does one learn what it means "to practice hospitality" if it isn't around your own table, in your own home, with your own family? We prayed together, we ate together, we talked together. It was natural that we should read the Bible together. You may decide another time works better for you than mealtime; I only recommend this because I have seen it stand the test of three generations. It is a workable plan.

Breakfast time suits our family for Bible reading best. (We usually are reading another book after dinner.) I dropped in at the close of dinner at my sister and brother-in-law's home

the other day in time to join them for their Bible reading —
five sons around the table, aged twelve to twenty-two. Dinner time works best for them.

Interestingly, we often reproduce the pattern we knew as
children in our homes. Even those who complain bitterly
about the deficiencies of their childhood family life often reproduce a pattern not noticeably different than the one against
which they chafed. Others swing a full 180 degrees away
from the past. Whether this is wisdom or rebellion depends
on the quality of the motivation and the goals which are
set. While it is easier for some to make intelligent choices
than others, parents *must* decide what quality of family life
they will have and then use the necessary discipline to accomplish this. Otherwise life will push the family in diverse
directions and they will be victims rather than disciples.

Ask a child if he wants to read the Bible after breakfast
and he may say *no*. Build it into the routine as naturally as
drinking orange juice and he will get proper nourishment.
One of my favorite cartoons shows a child in a progressive
school commenting to his teacher, "You mean *I* have to decide what I want to do!" When you are small and don't
know what is valuable, that is an agonizing responsibility to
place on a child.

I have mentioned the hindrances to family instruction at
length because they are very real obstacles. It isn't enough to
say, "Teach your children what the Bible says," thus adding
to the burden of guilt parents already feel. Presumably, a
fourth hindrance is that parents don't know how to begin.
Isolating the problem is part of the solution.

Sometime ago I listened to a panel of concerned Christian
parents discuss the matter of "family devotions." Several on
the panel mentioned their appreciation of the background
given them by their parents. Yet not one of the families was
successfully having any kind of regular biblical instruction
in their own homes. Their reasons will sound familiar.

They wiggle and squirm so much, we wonder what they get out of it anyway.

We are just never all together when there is enough time.

We have decided to wait until the children are older and want to participate more willingly.

We try to do something special every now and then.

I listened and thought of my grandparents. With ten children I'm sure it wasn't always convenient to read the Bible and there was plenty of wiggling. Grandfather probably didn't stop to psychoanalyze; he just did what he felt needed doing. I felt a rush of gratitude for a godly heritage. Because grandfather was faithful, my father was faithful, and we grew up in a home where we knew the importance and authority of God's revelation to men. We not only have a heritage; we are giving our children one. We decide what kind it will be.

But what if the father will not take the leadership? What if he is away from home much of the time? Many families flounder because of these societal patterns. The solution lies in the mother, who wisely takes over when she must, willingly passing leadership back to Father at the first opportunity. Don't cancel something this important while waiting for more ideal circumstances. A child's life is too brief! My own father traveled away from home much of the time, and so has my husband. Not to carry on with something as vital to life as this is like saying, "We won't eat any meals because Dad isn't with us."

I must confess to a personal reaction against the words "family devotions" or "family altar." Maybe it is because these terms have a sentimental, somewhat unreal flavor. An "altar" is outmoded since the death of Christ. "Devotion" is what we have toward God all day long, not just during a family reading together. I want to build more content into this family time than these words allow me personally. But what we call it isn't as important as that we do it! We simply refer to it as Bible reading.

But enough discussion about hang-ups which hinder us. Let's go on to a clear idea of our goal in Bible reading. Why is it so important? What are meaningful ways to accomplish it?

The Goal

The goal of family Bible reading is to teach children to think biblically.

That's a large goal: *to think biblically*. It means a good bit more than quoting certain Scripture verses. It involves squaring up our thinking with what the Bible says about God, about man, about sin, about redemption, about human need and righteousness. Thinking biblically insists on an understanding of the vast sweep of what the Scripture reveals to us. It is the square against which we measure our ideas and our lives.

How has God worked in human history? What is His goal? What is His essential nature, His character? What is the nature of man? What are his basic needs? How does the death of Jesus Christ fit into the picture? How do we know what is true? These are only some of the questions we answer in learning to think biblically.

The ability to quote salvation or assurance verses is inadequate unless they fit into a larger concept of the character of God and an understanding of His righteousness. Knowing favorite biblical heroes and specific stories are most meaningful when fit into a larger view of what their lives demonstrate about men or God's character.

Parents, not uncommonly, invest time with small children, reading them favorite Bible stories and speaking of salvation. The failure comes in teaching children through their teens how this information fits together to form a true philosophy for life. Our goal is a valid world-life view. This cannot be scolded into a person; we can only expose young minds to great Truth and discuss it with them. The rest is God's responsibility as He works with us in our children's lives.

Our need for a word from God is never finished. He speaks to our situation, ministers to our problem areas. We receive fresh insights, daily reminders, new promises because the Word of God is indeed profitable "for teaching, for reproof, for correction and for training in righteousness."

We demonstrate our confidence in the authority of the Word of God by the way we use it in our homes and by our personal obedience to it. No amount of emotional cozy feeling will stand the rigorous test of university exposure. Our faith has intellectual content; we must know what we believe. Emotional warmth flows out of the application and obedience of these great truths.

Attaining the Goal

In the bibliography under *Family Teaching* are a number of books to help make instruction in godliness a delightful experience for children. Beautiful, creative introductory books are numerous for younger ages. Begin very early to teach your children about God and His Son by reading these stories together.

Stories which relate biblical teaching to real life give opportunity for in-depth discovery as children grow older. Often questions at the end of the chapter give children the fun of remembering and taking turns. *Little Visits With God* and *Devotions for the Children's Hour* are only two of many other, popular and excellent books. Explore the list and make generous use of the material available. You'll find yourself learning afresh as you teach your children.

Primarily, however, I'd like to share the idea that has worked best toward attaining the goal in our family life. We have given this simple method thirteen years of trial and are pleased with its effectiveness in making the Bible meaningful.

FOR HANNAH

From *Prayer for a Child* by R. L. Field. Illustrations by E. Jones.
Copyright by MacMillan Company. Used by permission.

When our son Mark was four years old we began to read aloud from the *Gospel of Mark*. We chose this gospel because of its name and because of its short narrative passages. Father had a plan. Everyone at the table (and this included our numerous guests) had to ask a question and answer one. He made a game of it. Sometimes the question was directed to the person on our left, other times to the person on our right. We'd have to listen very hard, and sometimes the question we had thought to ask was usurped by someone whose turn came first and we would have to think of another.

At first our questions were simple. *Where did Jesus go? What did Jesus do? Who went with Jesus?* Mark picked up the idea rapidly. Then we began to interject another kind of question. *Why did Jesus say that? What does He mean?* And then later, *What can we learn from Jesus about the way we ought to act?*

In these questions are the three elements which open up any text: FACT — what does it say? INTERPRETATION — what does it mean? APPLICATION — what does it mean to me?

For a while Mark's questions centered on facts, but before long he began asking deeply penetrating ones. *If Jesus could raise Lazarus from the dead, why did He let His dear friend John the Baptist stay dead? Why did the Jews say Jesus had an evil spirit?* Increasingly we delved into the meat of what the text was saying.

Mark was delighted when Father introduced a two-part question, and thereupon set out to explore the possibility of a three-part question. Together, as a family, we dug amazing truths out of the Word of God — and no one in our family would say this was either dull or painful.

This method requires that everyone think through what the passage is saying. Ideas go through the thought processes and come out of the mouth. We experience a great thing: the joy of discovery. What is discovered for one's self is always more meaningful than being told by someone else.

It is exciting to see how the use of this method can become ingrained in a child's thought pattern and how this can enable him to take apart a piece of literature and comprehend what it is really saying. Children learn to listen, to isolate key ideas, to contrast and compare, and to come up with the heart of the text with the delight of a skindiver seeking a treasure on the ocean floor. Its benefits in our family have gone far beyond what we envisaged when we began this simple plan for Bible reading.

We have tried to handle the Bible honestly, letting it say what it says, not overly spiritualizing facts (which I believe turns children off because it lacks integrity and makes a sermon out of what isn't there!). The Bible is superb literature. It carries its own truth if we dig out the facts and apply them. We don't have to force its contents.

No need to attempt to protect Truth, to explain away seeming inconsistencies either. Truth will turn out to be truth. We've tried to relate the Bible to everyday happenings, school studies and new findings. When we've come upon words like fornication, circumcision, etc., we've talked openly about what these mean. If you have trouble explaining, look them up together in the dictionary. The Bible has adequate teaching about morality and sex for the twentieth century.

No other tongue in the world has the advantage of so many modern translations as we do! By all means, use contemporary English translations in your family Bible readings. So much of the message can be missed, avoided or tuned-out when Elizabethan English is read. The other day a woman said to me, "I like to stick with the original Bible." I didn't bother to tell her she would have to learn Greek and Hebrew to do that! The *King James Version* of the Bible was translated in 1611, and while its language flow is beautiful, particularly in the Psalms, young people deserve the privilege of hearing God's Word speak their own language in a twentieth century translation.

For those who are adventuresome, buy each member of your family an inter-linear Greek New Testament to read together as your family matures. The English words appear over the Greek words, and one family we know has taught themselves the basics of Greek in this fashion.

All of us want the Bible to be a living Book for our children. One truth seems overwhelmingly obvious, however. No matter what technique we use, our own attitude is the key. We must be *genuine*. Our blatant inconsistencies linked with outward piety will battle the authority of the Word of God in our children's lives.

If we approach the Bible with a stained-glass window voice and have emotional tremors that make the book seem "religious," in the most frightening sense of that word, chances are our children will escape at the first opportunity. Our prayers, too, must reflect that we are speaking with Someone who is Real, not making a speech.

The kind of family Bible reading I have been discussing is no rigid ritual that makes rules more important then people. On the contrary, it is because people, *people* God has given to us, are so *very* important that we are compelled to personal discipline in this matter. When we, as families, treat the Bible as "our necessary food," obviously respecting its authority by our own personal obedience, our children will find in this Book what they will never find in any other — the way of eternal life — without which there can be no lasting enjoyment of God's gifts.

I have talked about many books in the preceding pages, books which will enrich a child's life. If you think my emphasis has been imbalanced — that I have put other books ahead of the Bible — you are mistaken. For at least eighteen years a child lives in our home. If he reads the Bible with us every day, what conclusion will he draw from our emphasis?

You will determine your child's attitude toward the Book and books by the paths you open up for him. And it will affect your children's children and the free, imaginative communication of the Good News of Jesus Christ in the years to come.

*Books Your Children Should Have
the Opportunity to Enjoy*

Books Your Children Should Have the Opportunity to Enjoy

In the bibliography which follows, books are classified:

> General
> Poetry
> Christian (fiction, biography, missions)
> Teen Helps
> Family Teaching

Placing age categories on books is risky because maturity and reading levels vary so greatly. Instead I have given the longer sections three categories:

I. The young (generally preschoolers through grade 3)
II. Middlers, (approximately grades 4-6)
III. Teens and mature readers

Within each category books are listed generally from younger to older reading levels, thus enabling you to find your way through the listing of many books.

The annotations on the books are of necessity very brief. Each deserves far more enthusiastic comment than I've been able to include. I hope you will feel introduced to authors at least! (Naturally, the prices listed are subject to change — usually upward!)

The best way to use this guide is to take it with you to the library or the bookstore and browse around. Children's books are a wonderful education. I hope you and your children enjoy these as much as we have.

Notes: *VE*, various editions are available at different prices

The Caldecott Medal is awarded annually, since 1938, to the artist of the most distinguished picture book for children. The name of the award comes from Ralph Caldecott, the famous illustrator of books for children.

The Newberry Medal is given annually, since 1921, to the author of the most distinguished contribution to American Literature for children during the preceding year.

Bibliography

Bibliography

CLASSIFICATION: General I

Mother Goose, ill. by Tasha Tudor, Walck, $3.95.
   Seventy-seven favorite nursery rhymes with colored illustrations.
Book of Nursery and Mother Goose Rhymes, ill. by Marguerite de Angeli,
   Doubleday, $5.95.
   The illustrations make this book special. Contains 376 rhymes.
Goodnight Moon, Margaret Wise Brown, Harper, $2.95.
   A soothing sleepy-time story.
White Snow, Bright Snow, Alvin Tresselt, Lothrop, $2.95.
   Puts into words and pictures the marvel of a snowfall. Caldecott Medal.
Angus and the Cat, Marjorie Flack, Doubleday, $2.75.
   Angus is a Scotch terrier who has some merry adventures with a cat.
The Story About Ping, Marjorie Flack, Viking, $2.00.
   A little Chinese duck and his adventures of the Yangtze River.
The Tale of Peter Rabbit and 22 other volumes, Beatrix Potter, Warne,
   $1.50.
   Miniature books which are all-time favorites, illustrated by the author.
   Should be among a child's first books.
Millions of Cats, Wanda Gag, Coward, $2.75.
   A wonderful picture book about an old man looking for a cat.
The Snowy Day, Ezra Jack Keats, Viking, $3.00.
   A story of Peter's great fun in a snowy world. Caldecott Medal.
A Hole Is to Dig, Ruth Krauss, ill. by M. Sendak, Harper, $2.50.
   A collection of active definitions for pre-schoolers, such as "Hands are
   to hold." Also, look for *Open House for Butterflies.*

111

The Day We Saw the Sun Come Up, Alice Goudey, Scribner, $3.25.
   A lovely book which captures the wonder of sunrise. Look for A. Goudey's books on nature for older children as well.
A Tree Is Nice, Janice Udry, Harper, $2.95.
   Happy feelings about the delights of a tree. Caldecott Medal.
The Mr. Small Books, Lois Lenski, Walck, $2.50.
   Papa Small is proud of his three little Smalls. The series includes *Policeman Small, The Little Train* and others. Lois Lenski is a name to remember.
Mike Mulligan and His Steam Shovel, Virginia Burton, Houghton, $3.25.
   A race against time as Mike and his steam shovel dig a cellar.
The Little House, Virginia Burton, Houghton, $3.50.
   Story of a house in the country and the changes the years bring as the city moves closer. Caldecott Medal.
Make Way for Ducklings, Robert McCloskey, Viking, $3.50.
Time of Wonder
One Morning in May
Blueberries for Sal
   A favorite author whom your children should meet. All books are published by Viking at the same price
May I Bring A Friend? Beatrice S. de Regniers, Atheneum, $3.50.
   The King and Queen invite a small boy to tea and each time he brings one of his friends — a seal, a hippopotamus and lions. Caldecott Medal.
A Pocketful of Cricket, Rebecca Caudhill, Harper, $3.50.
   A pet cricket goes to school in a small boy's pocket.
And to Think I Saw It on Mulberry Street
Horton Hatches an Egg and many others, Dr. Theodor Geisal Seuss, Random, $2.95.
   Dr. Seuss' books are full of imaginative creatures and situations.
Five Chinese Brothers, Claire H. Bishop, Coward, $2.50.
   Five identical brothers who save each other's lives by one distinguishing trait each possesses.
Nutshell Library, Maurice Sendak, Harper, $2.95.
   Four tiny books in a bound set, full of fun and learning.
Where the Wild Things Are, Maurice Sendak, Harper, $3.95.
   A Caldecott medal winner by an author and illustrator to remember when looking for imaginative books.
Chanticleer and the Fox, ill. by Barbara Cooney, Crowell, $3.50.
   Chaucer's *Nun's Priest Tale* adapted by the illustrator. Caldecott Medal.
The Story of Ferdinand, Munro Leaf, ill. by Robert Lawson, Viking, $2.50.
   Story of a bull who favored smelling flowers to facing the toreador. *Wee Gillis* by the same author is a delightful story of a Scottish boy.
What Do You Say, Dear?
What Do You Do, Dear? Sesyle Joslin, ill. by M. Sendak, Scott, $2.75.
   Humorous handbooks on manners for very young ladies and gentlemen.
The Bears on Hemlock Mountain, Alice Dagliesh, Scribner, $2.75.
   A thrilling story of a boy sent over the mountains to borrow a kettle.
The Biggest Bear, Lynd Ward, Houghton, $3.50.
   Johnny wanted a bearskin on his barn so he went looking for the biggest bear. A popular Caldecott Medal winner.
Sam, Bangs and Moonshine, Evaline Ness, Holt, $3.95.
   The story of how a little girl learns to distinguish truth from "moonshine." Caldecott Medal.
Song of the Swallows, Leo Politi, Scribner, $3.25.
   Juan rings the mission's bells to welcome the swallows back. Politi's

illustrations have a warmth and gentleness appealing to children. Caldecott Medal. Also look for *Moy Moy* by the same author.

Madeline
Madeline's Rescue, Ludwig Bemelmans, Viking, $3.50.
    Inimitable Madeline and her adventures make for hilarious reading. Three other Madeline books are in the series. Caldecott Medal.
Hailstones and Halibut Bones, Mary O'Neill, Doubleday, $3.25.
    Delightful, imaginative poems about color enjoyed by all ages.
Two Is a Team, Lorraine and Jerrold Beim, Harcourt, $2.75.
    The story of teamwork and friendship of a little Negro boy and his white friend.
Ride on the Wind, Alice Dalgliesh, Scribner; $3.25.
    The story of Lindbergh and the "Spirit of St. Louis."
Winnie the Pooh
The House at Pooh Corner, A. A. Milne, Dutton, $3.50.
    Every child and adult will enjoy this lovable Bear and all his friends.

CLASSIFICATION: General II

Abraham Lincoln, Ingri and Edgar D'Aulaire, Doubleday, $3.95.
    Beautifully written and illustrated life of Lincoln from boyhood through the presidency. Caldecott Medal. Look for other d'Aulaire biographies.
Melindy's Medal, G. Faulkner and J. Becker, Messner, $3.50.
    Melindy, a small Negro girl, moves to a housing project from a basement apartment.
Charlotte's Web, E. B. White, ill, by Garth Williams, Harper, $3.50.
    A profound, tender story of a pig and a spider. A classic. Look also for *Stuart Little*, a story of the exploits of a debonair mouse.
Little House in the Big Woods and others in the series, Laura Ingalls Wilder, ill. by Garth Williams, Harper, $3.50.
    Stories of the Ingalls family told with skill — full of family warmth and the adventure of pioneer days.
The Moffats and other related stories, Eleanor Estes, Harcourt, $3.25.
    Lively adventures of four New England children.
The Empty Schoolhouse, Natalie S. Carlson, Harper, $3.95.
    The story of a 10-year-old Negro girl in a small Louisiana town and her loneliness and abuse as the first to integrate her school.
Henry Huggins and others, Beverly Cleary, Morrow, $3.25.
    The hilarious adventure of Henry, his dog Ribsy, and their friends. Look for *Ramona the Pest*, a female akin to Henry.
The Borrowers, Mary Norton, Harcourt, $3.25.
    A fascinating world of people no taller than a pencil who live in a quiet old house and borrow what they need.
Roller Skates, Ruth Sawyer, Viking, $4.00.
    A little girl explores New York City on roller skates in the 1890's. Newberry Medal.
Strawberry Girl, Lois Lenski, Lippincott, $4.50.
    Story of a little Cracker girl, full of Florida Lake Country flavor. Look for *Cotton in My Sack.*
Mr. Popper's Penguins, Richard and Florence Atwater, Little Brown, $3.50.
    Humorous story of a house painter and his pet penguin who becomes so lonesome that Mr. Poppers borrows a penguin from the zoo. A modern classic.

Thimble Summer, Elizabeth Enright, Harper, $3.95.
  The adventures of a small girl on a Wisconsin farm who finds a magic thimble. Newberry Medal.
Bright April, Marguerite de Angeli, ill. by author, Doubleday, $3.50.
  A modern story about a little Negro girl in Germantown, Pa. Also look for *Thee, Hannah!* and *The Door in the Wall*.
Heidi, Johanna Spyri, Macmillan $2.95, VE.
  A story of faith and hope — every child who reads this will love Switzerland and wish for a strawbed like Heidi's.
Peter Pan, James Barrie, Scribner, $2.95.
  The magical story of a boy who will not grow up.
Caddie Woodlawn, Carol Brink, Macmillan, $3.95.
  A redheaded tomboy and her brother have exciting encounters with friendly Indians on the Wisconsin frontier. Newberry Medal.
The Voyages of Dr. Doolittle and others, Hugh Lofting, Lippincott, $3.95.
  Wildly impossible and very funny adventures of a doctor who learned animal language.
The Secret Garden, Frances Hodgson Burnett, ill. by Tasha Tudor, Lippincott, $5.00.
  Three children find a secret garden and make it bloom again and the garden, in turn, changes the children. Also, *A Little Princess*.
Mine for Keeps, Jean Little, Little, $3.95.
  The story of Sal, a cerebral palsy victim, and her adjustment to family life after being in a special school. Exceptionally well-handled.
Little Women, Louisa May Alcott, Grosset, $2.95, VE.
  The classic story of family love, tragedy and romance in the lives of the four March sisters.
My Brother Stevie, Eleanor Clymer, Holt, $3.50.
  A story true to inner city conditions, movingly told.
Daniel Boone, James Daugherty, Viking, $4.50.
  A Newberry Medal winning biography of a childhood hero.
The Wind in the Willows, Kenneth Grahame, ill. by Ernest Shepard, Scribner, $2.95, Golden Anniversary Edition, $6.00, VE.
  Beloved Mole, Rat, Badger and Toad in their classic adventures. Look for *The Reluctant Dragon*, a tale of a dragon who preferred poetry to battle.
Twenty-one Balloons, William Pene duBois, Viking, $3.50.
  The adventure of a professor who sails around the world in a balloon. Newberry Medal.
Dobry, Monica Shannon, Viking, $4.50.
  A beautifully written story of family life in the mountains of Bulgaria.
Homer Price, Robert McCloskey, Viking, $3.00.
  Read the adventures of this boy just for fun.
Pippi Longstockings, Astrid Lindgren, Viking, $2.50.
  A little Swedish tomboy who has a monkey and a horse for companions.
Mary Poppins, Pamela Travers, Harcourt, $3.50.
  Mary Poppins blew in with the east wind to be nurse for the Banks children. Also read *Mary Poppins Comes Back*.
The Jungle Books, Rudyard Kipling, Doubleday, $7.95 (2 volumes).
  Exciting episodes with jungle animals written with powerful imaginative appeal. Also, *Just So Stories* for younger children.
Rabbit Hill, Robert Lawson, Viking $3.50.
  Small creatures — each with a distinct personality — create a warm, humorous story. Newberry Medal.
Silver Chief: Dog of the North, John O'Brien, Harpers, $2.95.

Lassie Come Home, Eric Knight, Harpers, $3.95.
Two classic dog stories every child should know.
The Little Prince, Antoine de St. Exupery, Harcourt, $3.75.
In a forced landing in the Sahara, a flier meets the Little Prince of Asteroid B 612.
My Side of the Mountain, Jean George, Dutton, $3.50.
A contemporary Robinson Crusoe, a small boy learns to survive and live with nature in the Catskills.
The Good Master, Kate Seredy, Viking, $4.00.
The story of a Hungarian tomboy who is sent by her father to stay on her uncle's ranch. Beautifully written. Look for *The Singing Tree.*
Freedom Train, Dorothy Sterling, Doubleday, $3.25.
The story of Harriet Tubman, the courageous escaped slave who devoted her life to helping others escape.
Wheel on the School, Meindert deJong, ill. by M. Sendak, Harper, $3.95.
Storks are brought back to their island by school children in a Dutch village. Newberry Medal.
Alice's Adventure in Wonderland, Lewis Carroll, Macmillan, $3.95.
An old favorite full of imagination and hilarious events.
Hans Brinker or *The Silver Skates,* Mary Mapes Dodge, Scribner, $5.00, VE.
Strong characterization, a complex and exciting plot have kept this book on the list of children's favorites.
Call Me Charley, Jesse Jackson, Harper, $2.95.
A realistic, well-written approach to the contemporary racial problem.
King of the Wind
Misty of Chincoteague, Marguerite Henry, Rand McNally, $3.95.
Marguerite Henry is considered by many to be the most successful writer of horse stories we have ever had.
The Complete Peterkin Papers, Lucretia P. Hale, Houghton, $5.00.
A series of amusing incidents from the life of the Peterkin family. A classic.
America's Paul Revere, Esther Forbes, ill. by Lynd Ward, Houghton, $4.50.
A story about a well-known hero which includes informative background to the Revolutionary war.
Bambi: A Life in the Woods, Felix Salten, Grosset, $1.95.
A book for 10-year-olds plus, this tender story shows deep respect for the wild creatures of the forest. It is often read too young in a popularized edition.
Black Stallion, Walter Farley, Random, $2.95.
A wild Arabian stallion and the boy who trained him. Look for others in the *Black Stallion* series.
Swallows and Amazons, Arthur Ransome, Lippincott, $5.95.
A small island creates a great summer adventure for two sets of English children.
Tales From Shakespeare, Charles and Mary Lamb, Crowell, $3.75.
A children's introduction to literature they will later meet.
Call It Courage, Armstrong Sperry, Macmillan, $2.95.
Story of a Polynesian boy's courage in facing the sea he feared. Newberry Medal.
Onion John, Joseph Krumgold, Crowell, $4.50.
Twelve-year-old Andy's dilemma over social pressure exerted on a simple immigrant vegetable peddler. Newberry Medal.
North To Freedom, Anne Holm, Harcourt, $3.50.
A boy who has grown up in a concentration camp makes his way across Europe alone.

The Matchlock Gun, Walter D. Edmonds, Dodd, $3.50.
Exciting true story of a boy who protected his mother and sister from Indians in the Hudson valley. Newberry Medal.

The Wishing Tree, William Faulkner, Random, $1.95.
The only children's story by Faulkner, the tale is about Maurice who sets out to find the Wishing Tree.

CLASSIFICATION: General III

The Adventures of Tom Sawyer
The Adventures of Huckleberry Finn
The Prince and the Pauper, Mark Twain, Harper, $4.50, VE.
Classics too good for any child to miss reading as Twain wrote them.

The Pond, Robert Murphy, Dutton, $3.95.
A story of a boy and a pond, written with great feeling and style about the pangs and pleasures of adolescence.

Smoky, Will James, Scribner, $3.50.
Written in western cowboy vernacular, this is a powerful book. If children are going to weep over animal stories, here is one worth their tears. Newberry Medal.

Johnny Tremain, Esther Forbes, Houghton, $3.75.
A novel for young and old about the American Revolution. Newberry Medal.

Shadow in the Pines, Stephen Meader, Harcourt, $3.50.
Fathers have been known to borrow this thrilling mystery from their sons. Good prose, fast-moving and exciting. Also look for *Who Rides in the Dark?*

Winter Danger, William O. Steele, Harcourt, $3.00.
No writer for children today can re-create wilderness life more vividly or movingly.

The Bronze Bow, Elizabeth George Speare, Houghton, $3.25.
Daniel's hatred of the Romans is turned to love by Jesus of Nazareth.

The Witch of Blackbird Pond, Elizabeth George Speare, Houghton, $3.50.
An historical romance set in Puritan Connecticut with a theme of witchcraft. Newberry Medal.

Carry On, Mr. Bowditch, Jean Lee Latham, Houghton, $3.50.
Fictionalized biography about an exciting historical figure of the 1770's. Newberry Medal.

The Yearling, Marjorie Rawlings, ill. by N. C. Wyeth, Scribner, $5.00.
Written for adults, but appropriated by children. A beautifully written story of a lonely boy, with superb illustrations.

Treasure Island
Kidnapped, Robert Louis Stevenson, ill. by N. C. Wyeth, Scribner, $5.00, VE.
Good writing, exciting plots — who could ask for more!

Call of the Wild, Jack London, Macmillan, $2.95, VE.
Adventure in the frozen northlands, a classic.

Big Red, James A. Kjelgaard, Holiday, $3.50.
Champion Irish setter and a trapper's son have exciting adventures together.

Old Yeller, Fred Gipson, Harper, $3.50.
A story of a fourteen-year-old boy and the ugly stray dog he came to love.

My Friend Flicka, Mary O'Hara, Lippincott, $4.50.
A boy, his mother, and a pony on a western ranch — a story which Americans young and old have taken to their hearts.

The Red Pony, John Steinbeck, Viking, $2.75.
When his pony died John discovers meaning to life.

Rascal, Sterling North, Dutton, $3.95.
Autobiographical account of the beauty of nature as experienced by an 11-year-old and his pet raccoon. Be sure to read another Sterling North, *So Dear to My Heart*, Avon paperback.

Moby Dick, Herman Melville, Dodd, $4.75.
An epic saga of the one-legged Captain Ahab who swears revenge on the white whale who crippled him.

Captains Courageous, Rudyard Kipling, Doubleday, $3.75.
A sea adventure, a spoiled English child who becomes a man, and Kipling's skill in writing.

The Sword in the Stone, T. H. White, Putnam, $4.95.
A humorous fantasy of the adventures of the boy who became King Arthur.

The Trumpeter of Krakow, Eric P. Kelly, Macmillan, $3.95.
A story of tense political intrigue in fifteenth century Poland. Newberry Medal.

A Wrinkle in Time, Madeline L'Engle, Farrar, $3.25.
Inter-planetary suspense and adventure. Newberry Medal.

Robinson Crusoe, Daniel Defoe, ill. by N. C. Wyeth, Scribner, $5.00, VE.
Read the unabridged edition of this story of a shipwrecked man.

Tessie, Jesse Jackson, Harper, $4.95.
A story of the conflicts that beset a Harlem teenager as she tries to reconcile two different worlds.

Adventures of Sherlock Homes, Sir Arthur Conan Doyle, Harper $4.95, pap. 65¢.
Hound of Baskervilles and others.
In Sherlock Holmes, Doyle has created a character so real that many think he actually lived.

Adventures of Richard Hannay, John Buchan, Houghton, Mifflin, $3.95.
A trilogy of spy stories, gripping, well-written and hard to put down. Skillful weaving of plot.

Ann of Green Gables, Lucy Montgomery, Grossett, $2.50, pap. 60¢.
An old favorite with girls, a book which has influenced many because of the simplicity and tenderness of the story.

The Thirteen Clocks, James Thurber, Simon, Schuster, $3.75.
If you haven't met James Thurber's sophisticated and serious humor, this is a good place to begin. You'll love it.

Jane Eyre, Charlotte Bronte, Dodd, $3.95, VE.
Wuthering Heights, Emily Bronte, Dodd, $3.95, VE.
The Bronte sisters spin quite different tales, both of which have remained popular through the years.

Up a Road Slowly, Irene Hunt, Follett, $3.95.
Talented and motherless, Julie tells of her growing years into high school. Reflective, excellent writing, good for certain kinds of girls. Newberry Medal.

Good-bye, Mr. Chips, James Hilton, Atlantic: Little, $3.50.
The moving portrait of an English schoolmaster and his three generations of boys. Also; *Lost Horizon*, Morrow, $3.95.

Kon-Tiki, Thor Heyerdahl, Rand McNally, $5.95.
Exciting account of the voyage across the Pacific on a balsa raft.
David Copperfield
Oliver Twist
A Tale of Two Cities, Charles Dickens, Dodd, $3.95, VE.
You will meet people in these books whom you will never forget and come to understand something of the history of the times as you read.
Born Free, Joy Adamson, Pantheon, $4.95.
A lioness raised among people is retrained for jungle life.
Cheaper by the Dozen, Frank Gilbreth and Ernestine Carey, Crowell, $4.50, VE.
Hilarious adventures of a family brought up in a house where father is an industrial efficiency expert.
Green Mansions, William Henry Hudson, Dodd, $3.95.
A romantic old favorite written in 1904. Look for Hudson's *A Little Boy Lost.*
Cress Delhanty, Jessamyn West, Harcourt, $4.95.
The story of a girl who grows up on a California ranch.
Northwest Passage, Kenneth Roberts, Doubleday, $5.95, VE.
The exciting story of a search for the passage to the Northwest.
Giants in the Earth, O. E. Rolvaag, Harper, $5.95, VE.
The saga of a Norwegian immigrant family in South Dakota in pioneering days.
My Antonia, Willa Cather, Houghton, $5.00.
A superb writer tells the story of an immigrant girl growing up in America.
How Green Was My Valley, Richard Llewellyn, Macmillan, $5.95, VE.
Beautifully written novel of Welsh mining villagers.
The Robe, Lloyd Douglas, Houghton, $5.95.
After the crucifixion, a Roman soldier wins Christ's robe and he is never again the same.
Anna Karenina, Leo Tolstoy, Random, $3.95.
A classic translated from the Russian which mature readers will enjoy.
Three Musketeers, Alexander Dumas, Dodd, $3.95, VE.
Story of three swordsmen who serve the king — an exciting adventure of their great feat in saving King Louis XIII from Richelieu's plot.
Les Miserables, Victor Hugo, Dodd, $5.50, VE.
The story of ex-convict Jean Valjean and his valiant struggle to redeem his past — a commentary on post-Napoleonic France, an adventure story, a spine-tingling drama.
Ben Hur, Lew Wallace, Dodd, $3.75, VE.
An exciting historical novel involving the life of Christ.
Cry, the Beloved Country, Alan Paton, Scribner, $3.95.
Moving and haunting story of race relations in South Africa.
To Kill a Mockingbird, Harper Lee, Lippincott, $4.95.
Beautifully written story of two white children in a small Alabaman town and of their lawyer father's defense of a Negro.
The Hobbit
The Lord of the Rings (a trilogy), J. R. R. Tolkien, Houghton $3.95, Ballantine 95¢ ea.
Tolkien is a superb storyteller. He creates whole new worlds, peoples them, gives them a language and a history, and takes his readers captive, young and old alike, into his adventures.

I Never Promised You a Rose Garden, Hannah Green, Holt $4.95, pap. 75¢.
  An extraordinary account of a teenager's battle with mental illness
  and the three years she spent fighting for freedom from her self-
  created prison of fantasy.
Black Like Me, John H. Griffin, Houghton, $3.50, pap. $.50.
  A white Texan, with skin artificially darkened, travels through the
  South in order to find out how it feels to be a Negro.
Ivanhoe, Sir Walter Scott, Dodd, $3.95, pap. VE.
  A novel full of adventure, romantic characters and suspense. Story
  of a noble young Englishman who lived in the time of Richard the
  Lion-Hearted.
Lord Jim, Joseph Conrad, Doubleday, $4.95.
  One of Conrad's most famous stories of life at sea. Underneath the
  excitement of his stories is usually a profound comment on the nature
  of man.
Bridge of San Luis Rey, Thorton Wilder, Grossett, $1.95.
  A Pulitzer prize winner, this is a story in which the characters are
  brought together in a common catastrophe and their lives thus inter-
  woven.
The Old Man and the Sea, Ernest Hemingway, Scribner, $3.50.
  Pulitzer story of old fisherman, who after a siege of bad luck, hooks
  the biggest fish he has ever seen.
Everything That Rises Must Converge, Flannery O'Connor, Farrar, $4.95,
  pap. $1.95.
  Excellent short stories for mature readers with a profoundly Christian
  message — the kind of stories that demand discussion.

CLASSIFICATION: Poetry

When We Were Very Young
Now We Are Six, A. A. Milne, Dutton, $3.50.
The Complete Nonsense Book, Edward Lear, Dodd, $4.00.
Stars Tonight, Sara Teasdale, Macmillan, $3.50.
Taxis and Toadstools, Rachel Fields, Doubleday, $3.25.
A Child's Garden of Verses, Robert Louis Stevenson, Scribner, $5.00, VE.
Under the Window, Kate Greenaway, Warne, $3.95.
Eleanor Farjeon's Poems for Children, Eleanor Farjeon, Lippincott, $3.75.
Songs of Innocence, William Blake, Doubleday, $3.50.
The Children's Own Longfellow, Henry W. Longfellow, Houghton, $2.75.
I Feel the Same Way, Lillian Moore, Atheneum, $3.25.
You Come Too, Robert Frost, Holt, $3.50.
Wind Song, Carl Sandburg, Harcourt, $3.00.
This Way, Delight (anthology), ed. Herbert Read, Pantheon, $3.50.
Oxford Book of Poetry for Children (anthology), comp. Edward Blishen,
  Watts, $6.00.
This Singing World (anthology), comp. Louis Untermeyer, Harcourt, $4.75.
Inheritance of Poetry, comp. Gladys Adshead and Annis Duff, ill. by Nora
  Unwin, Houghton, $5.00.
Poems to Read Aloud, comp. Edward Hodnett, Norton and Co., $6.95.
The Family Book of Verse, ed. L. S. Gannett, Harper, $5.95.

CLASSIFICATION: Christian (fiction, biography, missions) I

All God's Children, Pauline C. Webb, Revell, $2.95.
  Stories of children in other countries, told with warmth and human
  interest.

Suki and the Invisible Peacock
Suki and the Old Umbrella, Joyce Blackburn, Word, $2.95.
  Two stories about Suki, whose best friend is an invisible peacock, and her adventures. Imaginative, contemporary, spattered with valuable lessons.
Bird Life in Wington, John Calvin Reid, Eerdmans, $1.50.
  Fifty birds take on intriguing character to teach Christian lessons. Illustrated. Also look for *Parables From Nature*.
Little Shepherds of Navajo Land, Marian M. Schoolland, Eerdmans, pap. $1.00.
  Delightful story of Hesbah and her brother and the life of their people, with missionary emphasis.
Peter Piper, Missionary Parakeet, Gertrude Warner, Zondervan, $2.95.
  A parakeet, travelling with a missionary, gets into all kinds of adventures.
Susie's Babies, E. Margaret Clarkson, Eerdmans, $2.50.
  A classroom experience in raising hamsters helps present the facts of procreation in story form. Very well presented.

CLASSIFICATION: Christian II

Little Pilgrim's Progress, Helen L. Taylor, Moody Press, pap. 89¢.
  A simplified version of the famous Bunyan classic which captures the essence of its spiritual truths without writing "down" to children.
At the Back of the North Wind, George MacDonald, Macmillan, $3.95.
The Princess and the Goblin
The Princess and Curdie
The Light Princess, Crowell, $3.50.
The Golden Key, Farrar, $3.95.
  Written by the man who influenced C. S. Lewis and Tolkien, these books have a touch of the supernatural, much wisdom and reflect the quality of the author's life and other writings for adults.
The Secret Church, Louise A. Vernon, Herald Press, $2.50.
  Three children witness the persecution and struggle of early Anabaptists (new Mennonites). Fictionalized approach to history. Look for others *Strangers in the Land*, story of the Huguenots, *The Bible Smuggler*, story of Bible translator William Tyndale.
The Lion, the Witch and the Wardrobe
Prince Caspian
Voyage of the Dawn Treader
The Silver Chair
The Horse and His Boy
The Magician's Nephew
The Last Battle, C. S. Lewis, Macmillan, $3.00.
  These books are first in any class — superb storytelling, beautiful allegories, ageless interest. Mature 6-year-olds can listen, and adults won't want to stop with just one chapter!
Jungle Doctor Series, Paul White, Eerdmans, $1.50 ea.
  Titles *Jungle Doctor Operates*, *Jungle Doctor Attacks Witchcraft*, *Jungle Doctor Meets a Lion*, and a dozen others are exciting tales written by a missionary doctor. Told with the skill and flavor of a master African storyteller, these books appeal to all ages.
Jungle Doctor's Fables
Jungle Doctor's Monkey Tales, Paul White, Eerdmans, $1.25.

Like Aesop, Paul White uses animals to teach Christian truths, and give delightful reading.

Star of Light
Three Go Searching
Tanglewood Secrets
Treasures of the Snow, Patricia St. John, Moody Press, $1.95, pap. 89¢.
Children love Miss St. John's tender, adventuresome tales. As a missionary in North Africa, she writes *Star of Light* with understanding of the Muslim culture in Morocco, a book which should be read by adults as well as children.

Whistle Up the Bay, Nancy Stone, Eerdmans, $3.50.
Three sons of a Swiss immigrant are orphaned in 1870 in a small community in northern Michigan — a true story of adventure, faith, and initiative.

Swallow Cliff, Ellen L. Drummond, Moody Press, $3.50.
A novel of life in China by a missionary daughter. Little Swallow and Pony Boy are caught in a whirlwind of adventure.

Wilfred Grenfell, Joyce Blackburn, Word, $2.95.
Biography of the man who explored Labrador, a man whose adventures stemmed from his inner compulsion to discover and explore for God. Look for others in this *People-You-Should-Know* series.

Escape to Life G. Condor, Concordia, $2.95.
A contemporary story of a family's flight to freedom from East Berlin.

Nancy Hanks, Mother of Lincoln, Charles Ludwig, Baker, $1.00-$1.95.
Tom Skinner, Top Man of the Lords, James Adair.
Two books from the *Valor Series* of paperbacks about missionary heroes, men of faith from history and contemporary Christians. The series contains a variety written for juniors to early teens.

The Children's Crusade, Henry Treece, Penguin pap.
Exciting, fictionalized account of a strange historical event.

The Silver Trumpet, Owen Barfield, Eerdmans, $4.95.
A delightful tale of kings, queens, princes, princesses and a magic trumpet. Two sisters who look alike mysteriously represent the conflict between good and evil.

My Life and Baseball, Felipe Alou (with Herm Weiskopf), Word, $3.95.
Felipe Alou, a poor boy from the Dominican Republic, and his fabulous career in major league baseball. A reporter from *Sports Illustrated* writes this story of baseball and Christian faith with Alou.

Question 7, Robert A. Lee, Concordia, $2.95.
A story of the temptation and struggle of conscience in the effort to be a genuine Christian behind the Iron Curtain.

High Is the Wall, Ruth M. Berry, Fortress Press, $1.50.
The novelist deals with problems and disappointments of an interfaith marriage, attempting to handle honestly both Protestant and Roman Catholic positions. While not outstanding fiction, the story is informative and could be useful in a young person's life.

Me, Cazzie Russell, Cazzie Russell, Revell, $3.50.
An autobiography of a well-known Christian basketball player which may interest boys who like this sport.

The Will to Win
Play Ball!
Sports Alive!, James Hefley, Zondervan, $2.95 and pap. 95¢.
Sports heroes share their faith.

CLASSIFICATION: Christian III

The Screwtape Letters, C. S. Lewis, Macmillan, $3.50.
Letters from a senior Satanic majesty to Wormwood, a junior devil on earth, which cleverly pierce our Christian façade.

In His Steps, Charles Sheldon, Revell, pap. 50¢, Zondervan, $2.95 VE.
An old classic, dramatic and sentimental, but one which still influences young people on the question of priority.

By Searching, Isobel Kuhn, Moody, $2.95, pap. 59¢.
Vital account of a young person's search for God — realistic and well-written.

Borden of Yale, Mrs. Howard Taylor, Moody pap. 89¢.
The biography of a young man and the impact of God's character in his life.

The Gospel Blimp, Joe Bayly, Zondervan, $1.95, pap. 60¢.
Exaggerated satire on an attempt to evangelize a city with a blimp. Delightful reading, full of barbs which get some important truths across.

The Cross and the Switchblade, David Wilkerson, Random, $4.75, Revell, pap. 50¢.

Twelve Angels From Hell, Revell, $2.95, pap. 60¢.
Gripping account of one man's compassion in reaching street gangs and drug addicts for Christ in New York City.

A Man Called Peter, Catherine Marshall, McGraw, $2.95, Revell, pap. 75¢.
Stirring biography of a famous Scottish preacher, a man who became chaplain to the Senate.

Congo Crisis, Joe Bayly, Zondervan, $3.95.
Basically the story of missionary Charles Davis during the Congolese rebellion, this book gives a larger picture of historical significance. Excellent writing.

Jungle Fire, Bruce Porterfield, Zondervan, $2.50.
Actual experiences in contacting cannibal tribes in Bolivia.

Through Gates of Splendor, Elizabeth Elliott, Harper, $3.95, pap. $1.75.
The story of five missionaries who tried to reach the stone-age Aucas of Ecuador and of their martyrdom.

Jungle Pilot, Russell Hitt, Harper, $4.95.
Biography of Nate Saint who flew the jungles of South America, one of the men martyred by the Auca Indians.

The Dayuma Story, Ethel Wallis, Harper, $4.95.
The gripping sequel of the Auca incident, when two women missionaries return with an Auca girl to this remote tribe.

Tariri, My Story, Ethel Wallis, Harper, $3.95.
From headhunting to faith in Jesus Christ, a chief tells his story in his own way.

Through the Valley of the Kwai, Ernest Gordon, Harper, $3.95.
The bridge over the Kwai was built in less than two months by starved, exhausted prisoners. This is the story of a demonstration of Christian faith and the difference it made.

Another Hand on Mine, William J. Peterson, McGraw, $5.50.
A well-written, stirring story of Dr. Carl Becker, missionary to Africa. Highly recommended.

This Is My God, Herman Wouk, Dell, pap. 75¢.
A famous contemporary author gives an absorbing statement of his personal faith — an interesting look at Judaism.

Peril By Choice, James C. Hefley, Zondervan, $4.95.
A moving story of the courage and dedication of missionary John Beekman.

By Life or by Death, James C. Hefley, Zondervan, $4.95.
Missionary martyrdom in war-torn Viet Nam.

Does Anyone Here Know God? Gladys Hunt, Zondervan, $4.95, pap. 75¢
Down to earth biographies of contemporary women who have found Christ to be the answer to life's needs.

Devil at My Heels, Louis Zamperini, Dutton, $3.95.
True adventure story of an Olympic miler, full of exciting incidents from his life, such as 47 days on a life raft, two and half years in prison.

Pilgrim's Progress, John Bunyan, Zondervan, $2.95.
A fresh edition of an old classic every Christian should read because of the realistic picture of the Christian life given in it. An enthusiastic Foreword by Dr. Frank E. Gaebelein underscores the book's value to today's reader.

Hudson Taylor and Maria, J. C. Pollock, McGraw-Hill, $3.95, pap. $1.95 (Zondervan).
An outstanding biography of a real man who was also a great man of God and a missionary pioneer. Highly recommended.

Black and Free, Tom Skinner, Zondervan, $3.95.
Insights into the ghetto community and the negro church through the eyes of a converted Harlem gang leader.

Code Name Sebastian, James Johnson, Lippincott, $4.95, Tyndale Press, pap. $1.95.
A spy story with realistic Christian implications, involving a plane crash in the Negev.

Christy, Catherine Marshall, McGraw-Hill, $6.95, pap. $1.25.
A moving best-seller about a young woman who goes to teach in the Smoky Mountains and the mountain people she comes to love.

My Friend, the Enemy, William Pannell, Word Books, $3.95.
A negro evangelical attempts to "tell it like it is" and reflects his own struggle to find his identity in the black-white crisis. Highly recommended for mature readers.

For Us the Living, Mrs. Medgar Evers, Doubleday, $5.95.
A book a Christian should read because it gets inside the racial situation through the life story of Medgar Evers who was shot down outside his home at the peak of the civil rights battle in Mississippi.

Least of All Saints, Grace Irwin, Eerdmans, pap. $1.95.
Andrew Connington
Two excellent novels by a favorite Canadian author, thoroughly Christian, realistic, and well-written.

Servant of Slaves, Grace Irwin, Eerdmans, $4.95.
A biographical novel of the life of John Newton, beautifully written, moving through his life from slave-trading days to his influential ministry in later years. Highly recommended.

CLASSIFICATION: Teen Helps

Who Says? comp. Fritz Ridenour, Gospel Light, pap. 69¢.
What's the truth about the existence of God, the trustworthiness of the Bible, science and the Christian faith? This book tackles hard questions teenagers ask in a scholarly, popularized style, with additional references for those who wish to dig deeper.

So, What's the Difference, comp. Fritz Ridenour, Gospel Light, pap. 69¢.
A comparison of Christianity with major religions and cults.

Know Why You Believe, Paul Little, Inter-Varsity Press, pap. $1.25.
Thoughtful answers to some difficult questions, a book for a thinking young person.

Sometimes I Feel Like a Blob, Ethel Barrett, Gospel Light, pap. 95¢.
Short practical chapters on teenager's life, written especially for Christians.

Charming You!, Marjorie Frost, Zondervan, $2.95.
Helpful comments on making yourself more attractive.

Going Steady With God, Anna Mow, Zondervan, $2.95 and pap. $1.95.
A different daily devotional guide.

Why Am I Here? Where Am I Going?, Letha Scanzoni, Revell, $2.95, pap. $1.00.
Honest, straightforward answers with a Christian perspective.

Stand Straight and Tall, Bill Glass, Word, $3.95.
"A design for the man you want to become." Man-to-man talks for early teen boys written by a professional football player.

Altogether Lovely, Charlene Johnson, Fortress Press, $2.50.
Tips for the teenage girl on inner and outer beauty and grace.

Letters on Loveliness, Charlene Johnson, Zondervan, $2.95.
Practical hints on inner and outer adornments.

Find Out for Yourself, Eugenia Price, Zondervan, $2.95, pap. 95¢.
Encourages young people to think for themselves by facing up to the basic choices in life.

The Years That Count, Rosalind Rinker, Zondervan, $2.00, pap. 95¢.
Down-to-earth sharing about understanding self and Jesus Christ.

Tiffany's Table Manners for Teenagers, Ives Washburn, Inc., $3.00.
The world famous New York store presents its view of good table manners for young Americans.

Elbows Off the Table, Faith Coxe Bailey, Moody, $1.95.
Complete book of etiquette for teens.

Joe Doe, Disciple, Catherine Marshall, McGraw, $4.50.
"Sermons for young people" is not a description which does justice to the fine prose, the inspiring thought and the pull of these sermons by Peter Marshall.

Letters to Karen, Charles W. Shedd, Abingdon, $3.00.
Letters of wisdom to Karen about life, which have been popular in all circles.

Letters to Philip, Charles W. Shedd, Doubleday, $3.95.
Letters to a son on how a woman should be treated. Companion to *Letters to Karen.*

Your God Is Too Small, J. B. Phillips, Macmillan, $2.00, pap. 95¢.
Is your God old-fashioned, like a sneaky policeman? Every teenager ought to re-examine his idea of God with Phillips.

Guidance, Oliver Barclay, Inter-Varsity Press, pap. 60¢.
An excellent answer to the question, "How can I know God's will?"

How to Give Away Your Faith, Paul Little, Inter-Varsity Press, $3.50, pap. $1.50.
Clues, humorous, practical and biblical, to sharing your faith with others.

Mere Christianity, C. S. Lewis, Macmillan, $1.25.
With friendly informality, but with his piercing thoroughness, Lewis zeroes in on what he sees as the essentials in Christianity.

I Loved a Girl, comp. Walter Trobisch, Harper, pap. $1.25.
> A private correspondence between two young Africans and their pastor on sex and love. Enormous appeal.

Toward Christian Marriage, W. M. Capper and H. M. Williams, Inter-Varsity Press, pap. 95¢.
> A book about the privileges and responsibilities of friendship, the choice of a mate, self-discipline and other related topics.

Why Wait Till Marriage, Evelyn M. Duvall, Association Press, $2.95, pap. 75¢.
> This book builds a strong case for chastity, refuting arguments normally used to justify pre-marital sex. Also look for her *Love and the Facts of Life.*

A Time to Embrace, Oliver R. Barclay, Inter-Varsity Press, 60¢.
> A biblical view of sex in a constructive and practical presentation.

We Want to Live, R. Crossley, Inter-Varsity Press, pap. 95¢.
> Discusses purpose, value, love, freedom, success and God. Dynamic and relevant.

Take My Life
Consistent Christianity, Michael Griffiths, Inter-Varsity Press, pap. $1.25.
> Two books on practical Christian living, zeroing in on specific areas of daily life.

Quiet Time, Inter-Varsity Press, pap. 30¢.
> A brief, but ever so helpful guide to meaningful daily communion with God. Needs to be read often for fresh insights.

Sex and the Single Eye, Letha Scanzoni, Zondervan, $3.95.
> Provocative and relevant approach to a philosophy of sex.

CLASSIFICATION: Family Teaching

Prayer for a Child, Rachael Field, ill. by E. Jones, Macmillan, $3.50.
> Prayer expressing faith, hope, love. Caldecott Medal.

Pattibooks, Mary E. LeBar, Scripture Press, 60¢.
> *Sh-h-h, Who Love Patty? Joe's Strong Legs, We are Helpers,* and others for nursery age children. Colorful pictures on heavy, soil resistant pages.

A Stands for Angel
I Ask a Blessing
Our Father
If I'd Been Born in Bethlehem
If Jesus Came to My House
Seven Days, Joan Gale Thomas, A. R. Mowbray & Co., London, approximately 4/6 each.
> Simple poetry for the very young, delightful illustrations.

A Book of Good Tidings, Joan W. Anglund, Harcourt, $1.95.
> Fourteen favorite Bible verses illustrated in color by a well-known illustrator.

Fairest Lord Jesus, Frances King Andrews, Broadman, $3.00.
> Well-illustrated, the book uses short Scripture passages to tell the story of Jesus for beginners.

He Has Done Marvelous Things, Dorothy Andrews, Christian Literature Crusade, $1.45.
> Beautiful book that will help children learn about the creative, redemptive activity of God. Also look for *Everywhere I Go,* a book for pre-schoolers telling that the church is everywhere.

Hurlbut's Story of the Bible, Zondervan, $5.95, pap. 95¢.

Egermeiers Bible Story Book, Moody Press, $4.95.
Vos' the Child's Story Bible, Eerdmans, $6.95 (rev. ed.).
Richards Bible Story Book, Zondervan, $7.95.
  Four of the best-loved complete Bible story books. Compare them and have
  at least one of these on your shelf.
Arch Books, Concordia, 35¢ each, 2 ·sets, $2.00 set.
  The House on the Rock, J. Latourette
  The Little Boat That Almost Sank, M. Warren
  The Great Surprise, M. Warren
  The Baby Born in a Stable, J. Kramer
  and many others.
  Short, active stories, taken from the Bible, with colorful contemporary
  art. Great favorites.
I Wonder Why, Joan Summer
A Gift for Jesus, Joan Summer
I Saw a Mother Chicken, J. Ballard
Come and See, D. Kidney, Moody Press, 98¢ each.
  Four small books (ill. by Joan Summer) for small people with sen-
  sitive art work, delightful prose and rhymes, and simple messages
  about God and His care.
The Way of the Shepherd, Nora S. Unwin, McGraw, $2.50.
  The 23rd Psalm illustrated line by line through the story of a boy
  learning from an old shepherd.
I See Four
Two by Two, Mildred Krentel, Loizeaux, $2.50.
  The story of three men in the fiery furnace and Noah's ark, charm-
  ingly told.
Little Visits With God
More Little Visits With God, Jahsmann & Simon, Concordia, $3.00.
  Family favorites. Interesting, relevant stories which teach biblical les-
  sons.
Devotions for the Children's Hour, Kenneth Taylor, Moody Press, $2.95.
  Doctrinal teaching in story form, with questions at the end of each
  chapter for family participation.
Romans for the Children's Hour, Kenneth Taylor, Moody Press, pap. 89¢.
  A lucid translation of Romans with helpful comments.
Leading Little Ones to God, Marian M. Schoolland, Eerdmans, $3.95.
  A wide range of material covered, interesting and basic.
Living in God's Family, Mary E. LeBar, Scripture Press, $2.00.
  An excellent book for a young child who has just professed faith in
  Jesus Christ.
Teaching the Word of Truth, Donald G. Barnhouse, Eerdmans, $2.95.
  Creative lessons which teach great biblical truths by an exceptional
  teacher.
Our Father, E. Margaret Clarkson, Eerdmans, $2.50.
  The meaning of the Lord's prayer told in story form, designed for
  parents to share with children possibly 6 to 9 years old.
Climbing Up the Mountain, comp. Fritz Ridenour, Gospel Light, pap. 95¢.
  Getting the message of the Sermon on the Mount across to children.
Tell Me About the Bible, About God
Tell Me About the Lord Jesus Christ
Tell Me About the Holy Spirit, About the Church
Tell Me About the Lord's Prayer, Derek Prime, Moody Press, pap. 50¢.
  Well-done books designed to lend enjoyment to learning basic truths.

God's Church, DeVere Ramsay, Eerdmans, $1.95.
The dramatic story of how the early church took root, the men of faith in history, of pilgrims in America and present day missionary work. See also *God's Promises.*

The Church of Our Fathers, Roland Bainton, Scribner, $3.95.
Stimulating, highly readable history of the church. Wide age span, probably beginning with third graders for a read-aloud story.

Almost Twelve, Kenneth Taylor, Tyndale House, pap. $1.00.
Simple, but complete description of God's means for human reproduction.

How to Be a Christian Without Being Religious, comp. Fritz Ridenour, Gospel Light, pap. 69¢.
The Book of Romans in *Living Letters* paraphrase, combined with cleverly illustrated contemporary comment. Excellent for teenagers.

Men Who Dared, Barbara Jurgensen, Tyndale House, pap. $1.95.
Modern retelling of the exciting lives of Bible prophets (including text of *Living Prophecies*). An excellent, thoroughly enjoyable introduction to a section of the Bible most teenagers consider irrelevant.

Quit Bugging Me
Parents, Ugh!, Barbara Jurgensen, Zondervan, pap. ea. 95¢.
Two intensely interesting books beamed at teens.

Stand Out, an illustrated edition of *Acts* from Living Gospels, Tyndale House, pap. 60¢.

Come Alive, teenage edition of *Romans* from *Living Letters,* illustrated. Tyndale House, pap. 60¢.

Good News for Modern Man, American Bible Society, translation of the New Testament, pap. 35¢.